ZERO PREP

Ready-to-Go Activities for the Language Classroom

by

Laurel Pollard and Natalie Hess

Credits

Editor: Mary McVey Gill

Cover Art and Book Design: Bruce Marion Illustration and Design

Interior Art: Kathleen Peterson

Project and Production Editing: Aarón Berman

Production Assistant: Jamie A. Cross

Alta Book Center Publishers—San Francisco
14 Adrian Court
Burlingame, California 94010 USA
Phone: 800 ALTA/ESL • 650.692.1285
Fax: 800 ALTA/FAX • 650.692.4654
Email: ALTAESL@AOL.COM • WWW.ALTAESL.COM

Printed in the United States of America
ISBN 1-882483-64-2

Dedications

Laurel dedicates this book
To Adam and Geneva, who keep me on my toes
To Dan, who keeps me laughing
To Jackie, who knows (sometimes to my amazement) that I'm capable of anything.

Natalie dedicates this book
To John, my best friend and my knight in shining armour—
for everything

Acknowledgment

To our colleagues at the Center for English as a Second Language at the University of Arizona. Thank you for the many years of support, cameraderie, good times, and an endless exchange of ideas.

CONTENTS

INTRODUCTION 1

This Book..ix

INTRODUCTION 2

How to Use This Book ix

INTRODUCTION 3

Why We Wrote This Book...xii

CHAPTER ONE: ICEBREAKERS

1.1   Clearing the Decks 2
1.2   My Adjective 3
1.3   People We Admire 3
1.4   The First Time 4
1.5   Paying Compliments 4
1.6   What I Like to Eat 5

CHAPTER TWO: LISTENING

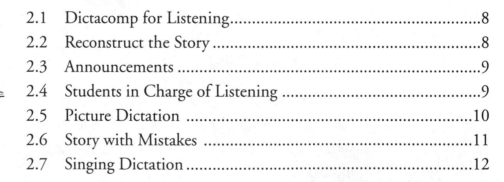

2.1   Dictacomp for Listening............................8
2.2   Reconstruct the Story 8
2.3   Announcements 9
2.4   Students in Charge of Listening 9
2.5   Picture Dictation 10
2.6   Story with Mistakes 11
2.7   Singing Dictation 12

CHAPTER THREE: SPEAKING

3.1   Find Someone Who 14
3.2   Candy Exchange..16
3.3   What I Need 16
3.4   The World Out There 18

3.5   I'm in Charge of My Own Learning 20

3.6   Building Up a Chain: Rules to Live By 22

3.7   Homework Review I: Seek and Find..................................23

3.8   Homework Review II: Homework Pairs 25

3.9   Homework Review III: Stand and Deliver 25

3.10   This Makes Me Think of That 26

3.11   The Birthday Line 26

3.12   Concentric Circle Talk 27

3.13   The Unfinished Story 28

3.14   Gossip 29

3.15   Two-Minute Presentations 30

3.16   Interaction Lines 31

3.17   Continuums..32

3.18   Role-Plays...33

3.19   Categories 35

3.20   What Machine Am I?...36

3.21   Real Language 37

3.22   Four Pictures Make a Story...38

CHAPTER FOUR: READING

4.1   Predicting from the Title 42

4.2   What We Already Know...42

4.3   Tell a Tale of Guesswork..43

4.4   Preteaching Vocabulary...44

4.5   Classic Jigsaw 45

4.6   Paragraph Jigsaw...46

4.7   Question Jigsaw 47

4.8   Vocabulary Jigsaw...48

4.9   Predicting from Sentences 49

4.10   Scrambled Sentences 49

4.11   Student-Made Tests 50

4.12   Find a Sentence 51

4.13 Change the Format..52

4.14 Telling Back and Forth 53

4.15 Reading with Half the Words 54

4.16 Overhead Summaries 55

4.17 Quick-Skim 56

CHAPTER FIVE: WRITING

5.1   Three Unrelated Things 58

5.2   The Classic Dictacomp.......................................59

5.3   Student-to-Student Dictacomp...........................60

5.4   Group-to-Group Dictacomp 61

5.5   Acting-Out Dictacomp.......................................62

5.6   Missing Words Dictacomp 63

5.7   Sentence-by-Sentence Dictacomp.......................64

5.8   Revision: I Can Do It Myself 65

5.9   Peer Revision I: What I Think You Said 67

5.10 Peer Revision II: Editing Written Work in Pairs 68

5.11 Quick-Write 70

5.12 Countries, States, and Cities..............................72

5.13 Remember the Picture 73

5.14 Written Argument 74

5.15 Gift Exchange..75

5.16 Who Is This? 77

5.17 Buddy Journals..77

5.18 Cloze Dictation 79

5.19 One-Minute Feedback 79

5.20 Faces...80

CHAPTER SIX: VOCABULARY

6.1   From Cold to Hot 84

6.2   Act It Out 85

6.3   Matching Words and Pictures.............................87

6.4   Words on a Chain 88

6.5   Going Shopping...89

6.6 Pointing-Out Fun..90

6.7 I Am the Curtains 91

6.8 Fashion Show 92

6.9 Poems for Students by Students 93

6.10 Two-in-One Vocabulary Review 95

6.11 Two Unrelated Pictures 96

CHAPTER SEVEN: STRUCTURE

7.1 Rainbow Teams *(various structures)* 100

7.2 Great Accomplishments Line-Up *(present perfect tense)* 101

7.3 All in a Day's Work Line-Up *(verb tenses)* 102

7.4 On a Special Day *(the preposition "on")* 104

7.5 "There Is Nothing to Fear but Fear Itself"
   (the preposition "of") 105

7.6 Verbs on a Chain *(verb tenses)* 107

7.7 If I Make a Million Dollars *(conditionals)* 107

7.8 Tell It Like It Isn't *(present continuous tense)* 108

7.9 Bingo *(various structures)* 109

7.10 Personal Questions *(question formation)* 110

7.11 Conjunction Cards *(conjunctions, negative forms)* 111

7.12 Truth, Truth, Lie *(question formation)* 113

7.13 Numbers in My Life *(question formation)* 114

7.14 Preferences *(present tense, adjective forms,
   question formation, third person singular)* 115

7.15 Sentence Contraction *(various structures)* 116

7.16 Sentence Expansion *(various structures)*................117

INDEX OF ROUTINES

INDEX OF ROUTINES 121

GENERAL INDEX OF ACTIVITIES

GENERAL INDEX OF ACTIVITIES 123

INTRODUCTION 1: This Book

(for people who don't have time to read introductions to new books)

What if you took the time to mentally review every activity that you ever used or heard of, choosing only activities that are the very best ones for language learning?

What if you then selected from that collection only those activities that take <u>no time</u> for the teacher to prepare?

We did that.

Here it is.

Enjoy!

INTRODUCTION 2: How to Use This Book

(for people who have a little more time to read introductions)

Do you spend time:

- preparing dictations?
- going through readings to find words that may be new to your students?
- preparing comprehension questions?
- correcting errors in sets of papers?

Using this book will help you spend less time on these chores and give you more time for creativity, planning, and vision.

The whole point here is to save you time, so we are not going to recommend that you read this book carefully from cover to cover. Instead we invite you to use the chapter titles and the indexes to find the activities you need. Our chapter headings will lead you to activities that concentrate on the four skills of listening, speaking, reading, and writing, as well as vocabulary and structure.

Our indexes will guide you quickly to activities for:

- class cohesion and energizing
- preview and review
- short activities
- pronunciation practice
- appeal to varied intelligences such as musical, logical, or artistic intelligence

A Special Note for Teachers of Languages Other Than English

The activities in this book are suitable for teaching any language. For the sake of convenience, the examples are in English.

Routines

A unique feature of this book is that it showcases routines. A "routine," as we use the term, is an activity so effective, so flexible, that we find ourselves using it again and again, varying the content and level but keeping the basic structure of the activity intact.

Some routines serve a specific classroom function. Brainstorming, for example, is an excellent way to generate ideas.

Other routines can serve multiple functions. Chains can be used:

• for preview or review ("Building Up a Chain," Chapter 3, page 22)

• to promote better pronunciation ("Gossip," Chapter 3, page 29)

• to energize a class ("Words on a Chain," Chapter 6, page 88)

• to practice structures ("If I Make a Million Dollars," Chapter 7, page 107)

Students respond well to routines because they feel they are on familiar ground: "I know how to do this!" Relieved of the need to figure out what they're supposed to do, they can plunge right in, giving all their attention to the language.

And routines don't become boring because they lend themselves well to variation in content, in level, and sometimes in the details of how we structure the activity.

Let's use brainstorming as an example of how a routine can be varied.

• Brainstorming can be done with any content.

• The level of difficulty can be changed by altering how much each student is expected to say or by allowing more thinking time before the brainstorm begins.

• A brainstorm may be done with the entire class, or smaller groups may brainstorm, with a representative from each group reporting their results in plenary.

An excellent way to begin using this book is to spend half an hour reviewing the routines. In the first index you will find the name of each routine and a description of it, along with referrals to the variations we have included as activities in this book.

- Do you use Dictacomps? Jigsaw activities? Perhaps you will find some variations here that you like!
- Are you curious about Rainbow Teams? Welcome to one of the best ways we have found to practice structures — and it's equally useful when you want to preview or review material!

A small investment of time in learning a new routine will pay you back a thousandfold!

A Note about Group Work

Throughout this book we have consistently used group and pair work because they produce a great deal of student activity and interaction. In a language class it is the students (not the teacher) who need to do the language work.

How we structure group work determines its success. Particularly in large, monolingual classes, students need to understand the goal, the task, and how much time they have. For example, much more effective than, "Discuss this in small groups" is "Together, work on these two questions. You have five minutes."

Students also need to feel accountable for their work in a group. It helps if they all sign any written product the group produces. It also helps if members of the group are responsible for specific tasks. These tasks may include:

- language monitor (keeps everyone in the target language)
- moderator (sees to it that everyone gets a turn)
- recorder (takes notes)
- reporter (presents group's results to the whole class)

A Note about Terminology

Throughout the book, we use certain terms that you will want to be familiar with.

chain: an activity in which students pass on information to other students. Sometimes they expand on the information, sometimes change it in some way, sometimes collect other students' information as it flows along the "chain" of students.

mingle: Students stand up and circulate with one another, talking "cocktail party" style.

scan: read quickly to find specific information

skim: read quickly to get the main idea

The Teacher's Tool Kit

Most of the activities in this book need no special materials. You can do every activity if you have a collection of "tools" that includes the following:

a dictionary

a thesaurus

some interesting pictures

index cards

a timer

a small box (approximately shoe-box size)

a stack of old magazines

a calendar

paper clips

INTRODUCTION 3: Why We Wrote This Book

(for people who just love a good story)

Our Experience

During many years of teaching, we have always tried to try to make our work better. Somewhere along the line we discovered the amazing fact that if we teach less, they learn more. And it is to this philosophy that we have addressed our book.

Laurel's Story

Laurel got the idea for this book during a week that may seem familiar to you, a week in which it was clearly not possible to do it all. Here is Laurel's story about that week:

I walked into my advanced class at the intensive language center feeling like the consummate professional. Having dealt with graduate students' needs and essential committee work as efficiently as possible, having postponed writing until next week (again), and having abandoned my exercise class weeks earlier for lack of time, I came to class prepared with a plan, a good plan, a plan carefully crafted to challenge and support every student.

The students had another agenda. A man had been shot as he withdrew money from a nearby bank machine that some of the students used regularly, and they needed to talk about it. Fortunately, I was willing to dump my plan overboard and follow their lead. Here is what happened:

- Students eagerly filled one another in on the details of the shooting (comprehensible input, information gap).

- Everyone had strong opinions about what is safe to do in our city and what is not (high-interest topic; language functions: interrupting, agreeing, disagreeing).

- Some students volunteered to clip follow-up stories in the paper for the next few days (student responsibility, skimming, reading for full comprehension).

- Students took some class time to write about the event in their daily journals (impromptu vocabulary exercise: key words on board).

- They finished their accounts of the crime for homework. The following day they reviewed what they had written, looking for the typical writing errors I listed on the board. Then they posted these accounts on the walls of our classroom for other students in other classes to read (self-editing, writing for a real audience).

I wished for more such classes. There had been no preparation on my part, yet a great lesson happened. Was I getting lazy? I doubted it. Instead I found myself remembering a number of activities that *minimize* teacher preparation time, *maximize* student responsibility, and *result in better classes* than most of my carefully crafted lesson plans.

I realized that a major cause of my too-long work days was overpreparation. I began restoring to my repertoire the zero-prep activities I had somehow stopped using—and looking for more of them.

When I got together with Natalie to talk about life and time management, I realized that she shared my point of view.

Natalie's Story

Here is a story that Natalie tells:

One of my trainee-teachers, Yoko (not her real name), was an unusually intelligent and conscientious graduate student. She had written brilliant papers on topics like code-switching, discourse analysis, and genre synthesis.

Her work in my course was also exemplary. Her lesson plans, unit plans, and journals were thorough and well thought out. Her class presentations before her peers showed her command of teaching techniques.

But when Yoko finally had to face a real class with real students, she fell apart. Ironically, it was the tension created by her wish to be perfect that destroyed Yoko's classroom performance.

When I observed Yoko, she was telling an attentive class about cultural differences in concepts dealing with time. One of the students, knowing that Yoko was from Japan, asked her, "How do people in Japan feel about time?" Yoko brusquely waved away the question with, "We don't have time for that right now."

She had tossed away a wonderful opportunity for real communication. Had she responded to this student's genuine curiosity, she would have opened the door for other students in this multicultural class to talk about how their culture views the use of time.

Like many of us, Yoko was too busy following her perfectly planned lesson to allow for real language and real human interaction.

Yoko's cooperating teacher decided to fail Yoko in the practicum. When I protested, "Oh, but she works so hard!" the cooperating teacher responded, "Who wants her to work so hard?"

He was right.

What We Have Learned

We wrote this book because we need it. We teach several classes each day. During each of those lessons we want to inspire, to motivate, and to create a mood for learning, growth, and communication. But, as we all know, there are days . . . and days. On some days we are inspired; on others we are just tired—too tired to plan a good lesson. We haven't even marked the three stacks of papers that are menacing us from the dusty corners of our desks. Still, there we are! The bell has rung. Our students expect us to function well, and they have a right to expect it. That's why we need this book!

The ideas in this book have helped us find time to grow as professionals and enjoy our teaching in a more relaxed way. We hope that using this book will help you free some time for the things that are really important to you.

We teachers are conscientious, hard-working professionals who often work harder than we need to or should. Everyone wants to be "good." Our profession draws people who feel that they are being "good" when they work hard, helping everyone who needs help.

Yet the essence of a successful classroom lies in having students do the work while the teacher facilitates. When we feel rushed and tired, we lose some of our awareness, flexibility, and creativity. Students inevitably notice. Enjoyment ebbs. Burnout looms. Students learn less. And all, ironically, *because* we tried so hard.

Planning vs. Preparation

Don't get us wrong: we are not recommending that teachers abandon lesson planning.

We like to distinguish preparation from planning. Preparation is what a teacher needs to sit down and do to get an activity ready for class. Planning is the vision we have—where our students are going and how to help them get there. Another important aspect of planning is before-class mental rehearsal—thinking through the branching alternatives in a lesson plan. Throughout our careers we need to construct lesson plans with branching alternatives. Doing this develops our ability to anticipate classroom scenarios. We also need to mentally rehearse how we will give instructions and conduct activities. This rehearsal gives us confidence and makes our classes go better.

While we will always keep the kinds of planning that do benefit students, we wrote this book to relieve teachers of the chores that *don't* benefit students.

What's Wrong with Over-Preparation

Over-preparation—working too hard—can spoil our teaching life in at least three ways:

1. Over-preparation can make us too controlling. We as teachers feel that we need to learn it all, know it all, use it all. Even when we have planned a student-centered lesson, the plan comes from our heads, not the students'. An over-planned lesson will inevitably make us less responsive to the moment.

2. Over-preparation can sometimes make us too busy, too teacher-centered during class time because we are wedded to a plan we spent a lot of time developing.

   When the teacher is over-busy in class, students may tune out, feeling exhausted, bored, and irritated. Material may go in one ear and out the other without "sticking." True learning, on the other hand, is exploratory. When we are relaxed instead of busy, we are more able to notice when students want to linger on an activity, explore something more deeply, or digress for a valuable tangent—even if this means we won't get to part of our lesson plan.

Less teacher activity goes along with more student responsibility and therefore more student interest, more student investment, and more student pride in accomplishment. (This, paradoxically, is why sometimes a spontaneous, unplanned lesson works wonderfully well.)

3. Being too busy makes us exhausted, less able to function creatively in class or to really notice our students. *And noticing our students is the key to good teaching.*

This book provides a reservoir of successful lesson ideas that need no preparation, can be done with ease and enjoyment, and give us time to notice our students.

Let Students Do Classroom Management Tasks

The underlying philosophy of this book is that *if you teach less they will learn more.* What we mean by this is that essentially students *must* take responsibility for their own learning. In other words, you can prod, you can motivate, you can provide excellent activities and excellent materials, but in the end **it is the students who must do the real work.**

In the area of classroom management, when we let students do some of the tasks we are in the habit of doing ourselves, we create an atmosphere of shared responsibility: "We're all in this together to learn," rather than "We're here to sit while the teacher feeds us language."

Classroom management tasks give our students the opportunity to be helpful (and often, to use the target language more). Meanwhile, we have gained some time to do more important things, like noticing our students.

Here are some ways students can help.

• Do you take attendance? Try this:

Tape a clean sheet of paper to the wall near the door. Divide the paper into two columns, headed "Names" and "Time of Arrival." As students arrive, they sign in. This helps reduce tardiness and relieves you of the tasks of calling roll and taking time out to note the arrival of late students. After class, transfer any notes you need into your book, then throw the paper away.

• Do you collect homework?

Establish a corner of your desk. Have students routinely put their work there.

Or ask a student to circulate, collecting homework.

- Do you

    distribute materials?

    move chairs?

    clean the board?

    copy something onto the board from your lesson plan before class?

    put things up on the walls?

    Let students do these things while you do something else.

- Do you review for your students at the end of class what they are to do for homework?

    Stop your lesson a few minutes before the bell. Ask students, "Do you know what to do for tomorrow?" A volunteer tells what the assignment is. Ask the class whether this is correct. Students offer additions or corrections. Call on another student to re-tell tomorrow's assignment. (If your plans depend on students' homework, a clear understanding of assignments is crucial.)

- Try this routine over a longer time period, too. At the beginning of a week ask, "What will we do this week?"

- Do you make announcements? (see the activity "Announcements," in Chapter 2, page 9.)

A Final Word

We hope that using this book will make life in the classroom more profitable and enjoyable for you and your students!

L.P.
N.H.

Chapter One

Icebreakers

Icebreakers are short opening activities that help to energize the class, release tension, and ease anxiety. In a language class, adults and adolescents may find themselves in an infantilized role that they perceive as distasteful and threatening. They have to learn how to function with a new set of language rules, a new lexical system, and even a new cultural framework. As a result, they may become tense and fearful, just when they should allow themselves to become relaxed risk-takers. Icebreakers are non-threatening activities that allow students to progress in language use while they get to know their classmates and together create a trusting and supportive class environment.

An icebreaker should:

- be short,
- be language-centered,
- give students a chance to learn about one another.

1.1   CLEARING THE DECKS

Students come to class with their heads full of personal concerns. Baltazar is proud of his new car. Gulnara hasn't been able to reach her family for three weeks. This easy, friendly routine for sharing "what's on top" helps our students get ready to pay attention and shift into the target language.

In this chain, students stay in their seats.

LEVEL: Intermediate—Advanced

AIM: Conversation, building a classroom "community"

Procedure:

1. Ask students, "How are you?" Invite them to think of a few good things and a few that are not so good. Tell them to choose one of each that they are willing to share with a classmate.

   Note: Occasionally a student may say, "But there's nothing good." Tell them, "I know life is hard sometimes, but that's when it's most important for us to notice what is good." Tell them that the good thing doesn't have to be big; little good things are just fine.

2. Give students a few moments to think. Ask them to look down while they are thinking and to look up at you to show that they are ready.

3. Count off the whole class, alternating A's and B's.

4. A's turn to the student on their right. A speaks first while B listens. Then B speaks while A listens.

5. A's turn to the student on their left. The new pairs talk and listen.

Note: Don't worry about the student at the end of a row. He or she will be without a partner half of the time, but will still be actively listening.

Variations:

1. In the second pair, they tell their first partner's news instead of their own.

2. In the second pair, they tell their own and their first partner's news.

3. In the second pair, they tell only the good news.

Note: This is one variation of a routine called "chains." If you haven't yet checked the Index of Routines, page 120 we encourage you to do so!

1.2   MY ADJECTIVE

This activity allows students to share personal feelings. It works especially well as a Monday morning wake-up.

LEVEL: Intermediate—Advanced

AIM: Class cohesion, learning adjectives, conversation

Procedure:

1. Ask students to contribute adjectives that describe people.
2. Write the adjectives up on the board and, together with your students, explain the words that some students may not understand.
3. Supply a few of your own adjectives, such as *sleepy, bored, tired, hungry, enthusiastic, happy.*
4. Ask students to pick one adjective that best describes them at this moment. Choose one yourself and explain why the adjective you have chosen describes you well at this moment.
5. Students mingle, telling each other which adjectives they have chosen and why it describes them right now.
6. In plenary, students talk about what a classmate told them.

1.3   PEOPLE WE ADMIRE

This activity allows students to share thoughts about a person they admire. It is particularly interesting in multicultural groups. Students reveal a great deal about themselves as they talk about the people they admire. It can easily be used as a prereading activity when the passage to be read deals with an admired personality.

LEVEL: Intermediate—Advanced

AIM: Class cohesion, conversation, practicing the relative pronoun *who.*

Procedure:

1. On the board write, "I admire people who _____."
2. In writing, students finish the sentence in as many ways as possible. (Allow only a few minutes for this phase.)
3. Students mingle, telling one another about the qualities they most admire in people.

4. In plenary, students talk about a person in their lives, a character in a book, a figure from history, or a famous person who has some of the qualities they admire.

1.4   THE FIRST TIME

This activity allows students to share a special moment in their lives with classmates.

LEVEL: Intermediate—Advanced

AIM: Class cohesion, conversation, practicing the past tense

Procedure:

1. Tell students to think of a "first" in their lives. It might be "my first kiss," "my first day in school," "my first lesson in a new language," "my first drive alone in a car," or any other "first" that comes to mind.

2. Demonstrate by relating a "first" of your own.

3. Students mingle, relating their "first" stories.

Acknowledgment: We learned this activity from our creative colleague Nancy Sciacca, who teaches at the Center for English as a Second Language (CESL) at the University of Arizona.

1.5   PAYING COMPLIMENTS

Giving and receiving compliments is a rigidly structured bit of sociolinguistic discourse. This activity helps beginning students to master the formula while they enjoy a little stroking.

LEVEL: Beginning—Intermediate

AIM: Conversation, class cohesion, practicing the present tense, learning how to pay and receive compliments

Procedure:

1. Teach students how to pay a compliment in the target language. For example, "I like your red shirt" or "I like your new haircut" or "I like your pronunciation." Teach the standard response, "Thank you."

2. Students stand. Ask them to look carefully at the student who stands on their right and think of a compliment they can pay this

classmate. Suggest several possibilities, such as "I like your smile," "I like the way you help," "I like the way you read aloud."

3. Students exchange compliments with their partners.

4. Students mingle, exchanging further compliments until you stop the activity.

Caveat: Be on the lookout for students who are not getting enough compliments and steer other students toward them.

1.6 WHAT I LIKE TO EAT

This activity gives students a chance to talk about their favorite foods. It works better after lunch than before lunch.

LEVEL: Beginning—Intermediate

AIM: Class cohesion, vocabulary extension, conversation, practicing the simple present tense

Procedure:

1. Ask students to name their favorite foods. Write all the contributions on the board and, with the help of your class, explain any new words.

2. Tell the class about your favorite food and when you like to eat it. For example, "I like chocolate ice cream and I eat it every weekend."

3. Students mingle, telling one another about their favorite foods and when they like to eat them.

4. In plenary, students tell about the favorite foods of classmates. For example, Tomoko might say, "Jorge likes ham, but he eats it only on Christmas."

Chapter Two
Listening

Teaching listening has often been neglected because teachers assume that students' listening ability develops automatically. However, listening for comprehension is an important aspect of the communicative process, and it needs to be practiced.

Students need to understand instructions, announcements, telephone messages, TV or radio programs, movies, and answers to questions they themselves ask. Effective listening is also vital in learning correct pronunciation and intonation.

It can take a lot of time to prepare interesting listening activities because students need well-designed input to develop their listening skills.

The activities in this chapter will help you to use listening activities effectively and communicatively—without preparation time.

2.1 DICTACOMP FOR LISTENING

This activity fosters concentration and encourages attention to detail.

LEVEL: Beginning—Advanced

AIM: Listening, writing, reading, review, preview

Procedure:

1. Choose any short passage your class has previously read.
2. Put key words on the board. Review their meaning and pronunciation.
3. Read the passage slowly while students listen. (They are not looking at the passage.)
4. Read the passage again at normal speed while students take notes.
5. In small groups, students rewrite the passage trying to get it as close to the original as possible. (Each group produces one paper.)
6. Representatives of each group read their passages to the whole class. As each group reads, other groups contribute corrections and/or additions.
7. Read the original passage again.
8. Students call out when they hear something that they had left out of their rewrites.

2.2 RECONSTRUCT THE STORY

Sometimes the simplest activities are the most adaptable and repeatable. This activity can be used for prereading or as a quick warm-up.

LEVEL: Beginning—Advanced

AIM: Listening, speaking, reading

Procedure:

1. Tell a story one time. Students listen but do not take notes.
2. Students write down three things they remember from the story.
3. In plenary or in small groups, students retell the story.

Extension (writing option): After the three steps above, students write the story as fully as they can. In small groups they compare their versions and write additions and corrections on their own papers.
Note: To use this activity as a preview, tell a synopsis of the longer story you are about to read.

2.3 ANNOUNCEMENTS

This routine turns everyday announcements into a challenging listening activity.

LEVEL: Intermediate—Advanced

AIM: Listening, speaking

Procedure:

1. Put students in pairs.
2. Tell the class: "I am going to announce some information to you. I will read the announcement one time. Listen carefully, then talk with your partner. Try to remember everything in the announcement. When you are ready, raise your hand."
3. Read an announcement about the class or school or something from the local newspaper. Choose a pace that is challenging but not impossible.
4. Say: "Turn to your partner. Go!"
5. When a few pairs have their hands up, get the attention of the entire class. One student retells the announcement. Listeners tell whether this information is complete and correct.
6. Congratulate the tellers.

2.4 STUDENTS IN CHARGE OF LISTENING

This simple routine can be used again and again with a variety of listening texts.

LEVEL: Intermediate—Advanced

AIM: Listening, writing

MATERIALS: A tape to play or story to tell

Procedure:

1. Play a tape (part of your listening-lab materials or a song or video excerpt that you or a student has brought to class). Or you can simply tell a story.
2. Ask, "How much did you understand?" Each student answers with a percentage number. Write on the board, 25%, 50%, 75%, 100%, to show students what you mean by percentage.

3. Suggest some things that students may want to pay attention to the next time they listen to the same passage. The listening text will suggest ideas to you and your students.

Possible things to listen for:

reasons
sequences
specific details
main idea
names
numbers

Put these or other things suggested by students on the board. Let students vote for one task.

4. Play the tape again and again, asking for the students' percentage comprehension numbers each time, until students tell you they've heard it enough times.

5. After each listening, ask students for a new in-listening task and note it on the board.

Extension (writing option): Have students take notes related to each in-listening task. Between listenings, students may compare their notes with classmates' notes (e.g., if the task was to listen for the description of a villain, students compare their notes about this). If there is much disagreement, play the tape again before adding another in-listening task.

2.5   PICTURE DICTATION

Using visual and written feedback, students help each other a great deal in this activity.

LEVEL: Beginning—Advanced

AIM: Listening, writing

Procedure:

1. Dictate an imaginary "picture" to your class. Adjust the dictation to the level of your class. For example, in a beginners' class it may be something like this:

"I see a house and some trees and flowers. There is a sun in the sky. There is a sick cat in front of the house. There is a girl beside the house. There is a road in front of the house."

2. Students listen to the description.

3. Dictate again while the students draw the picture.

4. In pairs, students look at their completed pictures and dictate the content to each other. This time they write the words their partners say.

5. Circulate, helping out with language.

6. Students post their pictures and descriptions next to each other.

7. Students get up to read the descriptions. They write additions, corrections, and comments on one another's papers.

2.6 STORY WITH MISTAKES

This activity provides a challenging listening task in a game-like atmosphere. Based on readings your students have done, it succeeds at every level.

LEVEL: Beginning—Advanced

AIM: Listening

Procedure:

1. Together with your students, recall a well-known story like "Cinderella" or "Snow White," or recall a story or reading passage you and your students have recently read together. Retell it with as many details as possible; ask the class to help.

2. Tell students that you will now retell the story quickly, making several mistakes. Their job is to listen for the mistakes.

3. Retell the story at normal speaking pace, making several mistakes.

4. In small groups, students tell one another the mistakes they have heard.

5. The groups report. The group that found the most mistakes is the winner.

Note: This activity offers great flexibility because you can adapt the mistakes to your class. You can make some easily caught mistakes to give everyone a feeling of satisfaction, and you can also make some sophisticated mistakes to challenge the advanced learners. Your mistakes can be in either content or in structure.

2.7   SINGING DICTATION

Even people who think they don't sing enjoy this activity. Not even the teacher needs to sing well!

LEVEL: Beginning—Advanced

AIM: Listening, pronunciation, spelling, grammar practice

Procedure:

1. Choose a song you know well.
2. Sing the first line. Students sing it back to you together. Work on pronunciation of important sounds as you go along.
3. Sing the first and second lines. Students sing them back.
4. Continue to build up the song in this way.
5. Students write as much as they can remember of the song.
6. Students look at other students' papers and revise their own.
7. You or a student writes the song on the board with input from everybody. Final help with grammar and spelling happens here.
8. Students copy the lyrics from the board.
9. All together, sing the song through once more.

Chapter Three
Speaking

Speaking fluently, accurately, and appropriately gives students the sense of security and power that they will need in order to communicate effectively in the target language. The activities in this chapter help students to take risks as they acquire language and to enter the world of meaningful oral communication in their new language.

3.1   FIND SOMEONE WHO . . .

This classic get-acquainted activity can be done with no advance preparation.

LEVEL: Intermediate—Advanced

AIM: Conversation, getting acquainted, practice with question forms

Procedure:

1. Write on the board a few examples of information students might want to learn about classmates. Leave a blank before each item. Here are a few possibilities to choose from. You will, of course, have your own ideas about what your students want to know about each other.

   Find someone who . . .

   _____ has more than five brothers and sisters.

   _____ was born in this city.

   _____ knows how to use the bus system.

   _____ came here less than three days ago.

   _____ has a car.

   _____ knows how to fix a car.

   _____ likes to dance.

   _____ is married.

   _____ is a good cook.

   _____ thinks that learning a new language is easy.

   _____ thinks that learning a new language can be fun.

   _____ is worried today.

   _____ has some good news to share.

   _____ needs the target language for their work.

   _____ needs the target language for school.

   _____ would rather be somewhere else.

2. Ask students what they want to know about classmates. Add their ideas to the list.

3. Students copy the list from the board, including the blank spaces.

4. Put question "frames" on the board, for example,

    "How many _____ do you have?"

    "Do you have/like/want/know/need _____?"

    "Are you _____?"

5. Lead the class in choral practice of the questions they will be asking. For example:

    "How many brothers and sisters do you have?"

6. Students stand and pair up with other students. Each partner asks the other about only one item. If the answer is "Yes," the asker writes the answerer's name in the blank on the list.

    Note: These exchanges should be brief. However, if students find an exchange particularly interesting, they may linger a bit to find out more. For example: "Oh, you're worried today? What about?" "You need this new language for your work? What do you do?"

7. Each student thanks the first partner and finds a second one. The activity continues as long as students are actively enjoying it.

8. Circulate during the game. If you hear errors in question formation, invite the asker to look at the question frames on the board and try again.

9. In plenary, ask students to tell the most interesting thing they learned about a classmate.

Extension: Hand out pieces of tape so students can tape their lists up around the room. Students walk around, learning about classmates from the lists and talking with each other.

Variation: If you want your students to practice forming yes/no questions, demonstrate by asking a volunteer to question you about something on the board before everyone stands and mingles. Tell this volunteer that you will answer only "Yes" or "No." (If the student says, for example, "How many brothers and sisters do you have?," just smile and answer, "Yes!" Classmates may help until everyone gets the point.) Again, put question frames on the board. For example:

"Do you have/want/like/know _____?"

"Are you _____?"

3.2   CANDY EXCHANGE

This activity offers a sweet get-acquainted strategy.

LEVEL: Intermediate—Advanced

AIM: Speaking, getting to know one another

MATERIALS: A bag of quickly eaten candies (sweets)

Procedure:

1. Give each student three pieces of candy.

2. Students get up and mingle. Each student shares one fact about himself or herself with one other student and is then allowed to eat one candy.

3. Students change partners and repeat Step 2.

4. They repeat the procedure with a third partner.

5. Students sit down.

6. In plenary, students tell what they remember about one another.

7. The student who remembers the most facts about the most students gets the remainder of the candy. If there is a tie, two students split the loot.

3.3   WHAT I NEED

Whatever you need, if you gather a group of ten people and announce your need, you will probably find help—either directly from one of the ten or indirectly from someone that they refer you to.

Students who have recently arrived in a new place may feel "disconnected" until they establish new routines. Classmates can help. This activity brings students' real concerns into the classroom. As they ask for and receive help, a climate of cohesion, friendliness, and trust develops.

LEVEL: Intermediate—Advanced

AIM: Class cohesion, conversation, solving problems

Procedure:

1. Ask students what they need. If necessary, mention one or two things you think your students might need. Our students, for example, have mentioned these needs:

a driver's license

a grocery store that sells food from their country

a native speaker to practice with

a place to live with cheaper rent

a ride to a lumberyard to pick up a piece of plywood to put under a soft mattress

2. Students write what they need on a piece of paper. Encourage them to write more than one need.

3. Students read these papers aloud one by one. As classmates listen, they raise their hands if they think they can help. The reader writes down these names.

   Note: In larger groups, post all the papers around the room. Students circulate, reading every paper and writing their names by all the needs they think they can help with.

4. Students mingle, talking with classmates who might be able to help them, gathering information and making plans.

5. In plenary, volunteers tell what help they have found. This is exciting because people often feel that they are alone with their problems. This activity helps dispel that discouragement.

Extensions:

1. In a later lesson, students who have received help write or give short oral presentations about what has happened.

2. Students who have given help write or give oral presentations about what they did. The act of giving help is a fine remedy for students who feel powerless or unimportant. (And don't we all, from time to time?)

3.4   THE WORLD OUT THERE

We know that our lessons can go only so far in bridging students from classroom language to real-world language. Even if you are teaching in a country that uses the language you are teaching, some students do not use the language much outside of class. In settings where your students cannot go out and use the target language, the challenges are even greater. Here are some ideas to maximize students' use of their new language beyond the classroom.

LEVEL: Intermediate—Advanced

AIM: Improving speaking and listening ability

Procedure:

1. Ask students if they would like to make much faster progress in listening and speaking in the target language without attending extra classes, doing extra homework, or studying more.

2. Tell them that the key is applying their classroom learning in real situations.

3. Ask what they already do to use the target language outside of class. Students might mention listening to conversations in restaurants, watching TV, or asking for directions.

    Put a few of these ideas on the board and brainstorm some more ideas about what they might do. One good way to brainstorm follows.

    a. Everyone thinks for sixty seconds.
    b. Two or three students go to the board. They will take turns writing what they hear, so that every idea is noted on the board.
    c. Keeping the pace rapid, call on students one after another. Each calls out an idea. Everyone must listen carefully, because they can't repeat an idea that was offered earlier. Take an occasional turn yourself.
    d. If a student has no idea to offer, he or she says, "Pass." Tell students, "Passing is OK. You might have a new idea the next time I call on you."

e. When ten students in a row say, "Pass," the brainstorm is almost finished. Ask whether any volunteers have any last ideas to offer.

f. Read the ideas from the board aloud or have a student who reads and speaks well read them. Now your brainstorm is finished.

4. Students come up to the board and write a checkmark next to the three ideas they would most like to do.

5. (if time allows) Choose one or more of the most popular ideas. Generate lists of things students might say in those situations. For example, if many students have checked "pretend to be shopping and ask a clerk for help," you might elicit from students such phrases as:

"Excuse me, where is/are the _____?"
"Do you have this in another size/color?"
"Thanks for your help! I think I'll check a couple of other places before making up my mind."

6. Each student chooses one idea for homework. Tell students that they may do this singly or in pairs. If they want a partner, help them find one during class time.

7. Each student gives you a note that looks like this:

"I, _____(name), will_____(activity) sometime during the next _____ days."

8. Students later report on their results, orally or in writing. The report should include:

what they did,
where they did it,
how they felt about it,
what words or phrases they want to remember.

Following are some ideas that have worked well for our students. Some work as whole-class activities; all can be done by individuals or pairs of students. Students can:

1. go to a museum. They pretend to be tourists who speak the target language, asking questions and remarking to other museum patrons about what they see. This activity works well if you are teaching English as a foreign language in a non-English speaking country.

2. observe classes in schools in your area where your target language is the language of instruction

3. go to lectures, poetry readings, club meetings, political speeches, etc.

4. watch TV

5. listen to radio talk shows

6. listen to songs over and over. Write down the words. Sing them.

7. chat with people who aren't very busy:

    a. at bus stops (After a nice chat with someone waiting for a bus, it's easy to say, "This isn't my bus. Nice talking with you! So long!")

    b. while riding the bus

    c. waiting in lines

    d. in cafeteria-style restaurants

8. ask for help:

    a. in stores (pretend to be shopping)

    b. in banks

9. use the telephone to get information such as:

    a. movie times

    b. weather report

    c. airplane schedules

    d. business/museum hours

3.5   I'M IN CHARGE OF MY OWN LEARNING

The most successful students know that they are in charge of their own learning. This activity can shift all your students in that direction.

LEVEL: Intermediate—Advanced

AIM: Increasing student self-direction

Procedure:

1. Ask students what they want to learn in your class and why. For example, students may mention needing more vocabulary, improving their pronunciation, or learning grammar.

2. Each student turns a piece of paper sideways and draws lines to make four columns. In each column, students write the following headings:

What I want to do in my new language	Why I need to do this	What I do now to improve my skill	Other things I could do

3. In pairs, students have a conversation about all four columns, filling in their own charts as they go along. This allows students to get to know each other better.

Here is an example of what one student wrote:

What I want to do in my new language:	Why I need to do this:	What I do now to improve my skill :	Other things I could do:
I want to learn a lot of words.	Because I want to understand movies.	I write new words in my notebook with translations.	I could use my new words in conversation more often.
I want to improve my listening.	Because I can't understand my child's teacher very well when we meet.	I listen to my teacher as well as I can.	I could go to the listening lab and use the tapes there. I could also tape a TV show and watch it over and over.

4. Pairs take pairs. In these new groups of four, students tell each other their ideas. Encourage students to "borrow" freely; if they hear an idea they like, they may add it to their own chart.

5. In plenary, volunteers share some good ideas. These can be their own ideas or ones they heard from classmates.

Extensions:

1. Students can write notes to each other as the course progresses, describing how they are taking charge of their own learning. These can be posted on a public bulletin board for others in the school to read.

2. Students can report their successes to you in a weekly journal.

3. Students can share their stories orally. (See "Concentric Circle Talk" in this chapter, page 27, for one good way to do this.)

3.6   BUILDING UP A CHAIN: RULES TO LIVE BY

This activity is an efficient way for students to share information and ideas. It challenges memory and keeps every student active. It is very effective in content-based classes.

LEVEL: Intermediate—Advanced

AIM: Giving and receiving information orally

Procedure:

1. Ask students, "What are three important rules to live by, three things that all children should learn about in order to live a good life?"

2. Each student writes three rules.

3. Students mingle. Each student tells their first partner their three rules and listens to the partner's rules.

4. Students move on to a second partner. They tell their original three rules plus one that they just heard from their first partners (total of four). They also hear four rules from their second partners.

5. With the third partner, each student tells the same four rules and adds a new one he or she heard from the second partner. (The total is now five.)

6. Continue the activity until memory breaks down and the students give up. (Students sometimes amaze us with how much they can remember.)

7. In plenary, find out who has the longest list and invite that student to come to the front of the class and recite his/her list.

8. Ask everyone what rules they encountered most frequently during the activity. List these on the board. Do not organize this list.

9. In small groups, students combine the rules they think are similar, eliminate unimportant ones, and put the others in order from *most* important to *least* important. A group secretary writes the list. A spokesperson from each group reads these to the whole class.

Note: This routine is also useful for:

1. *brainstorming (e.g., What are some good ways to practice the target language outside of class?)*

2. *previewing (e.g., What animals do you think we will see when we go to the zoo?)*

3. *reviewing (e.g., What do we remember from the article we read yesterday?)*

4. *vocabulary (e.g., How many words do we know that are associated with travel?)*

3.7 HOMEWORK REVIEW I: SEEK AND FIND

Correcting a set of homework papers one by one is not the most valuable use of a teacher's time. This and the following two activities are three options that free you for more important work while giving your students immediate feedback on the work they have done at home.

LEVEL: Beginning—Advanced

AIM: Speaking (polite disagreement), correcting homework assignments, learning from peers

Procedure:

1. Distribute an answer key or simply read out the correct answers.

2. Students check their own homework papers, circling items they got wrong.

3. Everyone stands and mingles, looking for papers that have correct answers to those items.

4. When they find a classmate who answered correctly, they discuss that item.

5. When they are satisfied about why this other answer is correct, they move on to look for new partners.

6. When most students are finished, stop the activity.

Note: When you want to know how individual students did on a homework assignment, collect the papers. Encourage students not to erase and change their incorrect answers during the activity, but to circle their errors so that you can see where they need help and plan lessons that will help them.

Extension: Correct answers are proof that a student can already do something. Errors are more exciting and useful than correct answers because they point to what a student can learn next. This extension keeps students at what Vygotsky has called "the edge of learning." It promotes students' ability to analyze and improve their own reading strategies. A good way to extend this activity is as follows:

1. After students have done the six steps above, they sit down.

2. Circulate, pointing at one circled answer on each student's paper. The student writes a note about why this first answer was not correct. This promotes student accountability; if they have analyzed each of their errors, they can easily write an explanation for the error you choose.

   Alternatively, ask students to choose one error on their own, an error that has taught them something important about how to read better.

For example, students may write:

   "I didn't check statement #4 because I don't think it's true. But the exercise asks for the <u>author's</u> opinion, not <u>mine</u>. I need to keep thinking while I'm reading, but I shouldn't mix up my ideas with the author's."

   "I didn't understand the directions. I need to read directions carefully, even if it takes extra time."

3. Collect these notes.

Note: This activity creates some homework for you, but it is a good "spot-check" of what students are teaching themselves about how to read better. For each short note you collect, the student has worked hard to analyze a number of errors; in other words, you are seeing the tip of the iceberg.

3.8 HOMEWORK REVIEW II: HOMEWORK PAIRS

LEVEL: Beginning—Advanced

AIM: Speaking (polite disagreement), correcting homework assignments, learning from peers

Procedure:

1. In pairs, students compare their answers to a homework assignment. When they disagree on an answer, they try to persuade each other.

2. If they still do not agree, they ask for your help or walk around to learn other pairs' opinions.

Note: To promote students' analysis of their errors, use the extension activity in "Homework Review I: Seek and Find," page 23.

3.9 HOMEWORK REVIEW III: STAND AND DELIVER

LEVEL: Beginning—Advanced

AIM: Speaking (polite disagreement), correcting homework assignments, learning from peers

Procedure:

1. One student stands up and reads his/her answers aloud as classmates check their homework.

2. Any student who has a different answer calls out, "Wait!"

3. The reader and the challenger defend their answers. (Other students may also contribute to this discussion.)

4. The student who successfully defends the correct answer wins the right to continue the activity by standing and reading his/her next answer.

Notes:

1. *This can be quite lively and fun, as students vie for the right to be the next reader and vigorously defend their answers.*

2. *To promote students' analysis of their errors, use the extension activity in "Homework Review I: Seek and Find," page 23.*

3.10   THIS MAKES ME THINK OF THAT

This activity fosters creativity and promotes interesting conversation.

LEVEL: Intermediate—Advanced

AIM: Speaking

Procedure:

1. Students sit in a circle.

2. Appoint a secretary/challenger. This person will write student responses on the board and later challenge students to validate their responses.

3. Say any word—for example, "Money."

4. The student on your right says the first thing that comes to his or her mind when he or she thinks of money—for example, "Power."

5. The next student continues; e.g., "Napoleon."

6. The following student might say, "Josephine."

7. The next student could say, "Jimmy."

8. The following student might say, "Carter."

9. A student who can't think of anything may say, "Pass," and the chain will continue.

10. The chain continues until enthusiasm lags.

11. The challenger may stop the chain at any time to ask the student who has given a response to validate it. For example: "Lucinda, why did Josephine make you think of Jimmy?"

12. Students explain their reactions; for example, "They both begin with *J*, don't they?" Other students may question and add their own associations.

3.11   THE BIRTHDAY LINE

This is a fine get-acquainted activity that promotes lively conversation.

LEVEL: Intermediate—Advanced

AIM: Fluency, listening, getting to know one another

Procedure:

1. Appoint two to three students who will serve as the "gossips." They will circulate among the other students and try to learn as much information as possible.

2. All students except for the "gossips" line up according to their birthdays, starting with students born in January at one end of the room and moving on to students born in December.

3. In order, students call out their birthdays (e.g., January 22nd) to make sure the line is in the right order. They change places if necessary.

4. Staying in line, students turn to a partner and describe how they like (or would like) to celebrate their birthdays.

5. Students turn to new partners to tell what they have learned from their previous partners.

6. The "gossips" circulate and listen.

7. In plenary, the "gossips" report to the class what they overheard. Expect lots of laughter and good fun.

Note: Line-ups can also be used with other topics, such as who comes to school earliest, who stays up latest, or who has lived in one place the longest.

Caveat: Avoid topics that might make some students feel less important than others.

CONCENTRIC CIRCLE TALK

We use this activity again and again in our classes. It pushes students to say more than they believed possible. It can be used with any content and at any level.

LEVEL: Beginning—Advanced

AIM: Speaking, listening, preview and review, pre-writing

Procedure:

1. Choose a subject you want students to talk about: a dream, future plans, most frightening experience, etc. (You could also tailor the topic to class content.)

2. Students stand in two concentric circles. Each inner-circle student is facing an outer-circle partner.

3. Give students one minute to plan what they will say when their turn comes.

4. The inner-circle students speak first. Say, "You have three minutes to talk. There's only one rule: *Don't stop talking*. If you finish early, start over again. If you can't think of the right word, say it a different way. If you don't have ideas, say, 'Ba, ba, ba, . . .' Sooner or later an idea will come to you. But *don't stop talking*."

5. Tell the listening partners in the outer circle, "Your job is very important. This is not a conversation, so don't ask questions or talk at all. Just lean forward, let your face show that you are very interested, and listen to your partner."

6. At your signal (clapping hands works well), all inner-circle students talk simultaneously while their partners listen.

7. At the end of three minutes, signal again for speakers to stop. (Invite listeners to thank their speakers after each phase of this activity.)

8. Speakers move one place to their right. Now they tell the same thing to their new partners in two minutes.

9. They move one place to the right again and tell the same thing to a third partner in one minute. Speakers will have to edit and talk even faster this time!

10. Repeat Steps 5–9 with the outer circle as speakers. They will rotate to their right to find new partners.

11. In plenary, ask students whether they enjoyed this activity and why. Invite volunteers to tell something they heard from one of their speaking partners.

Variation: Start with one minute, then expand the time to two, then three minutes. This allows students to elaborate rather than condense and edit.

3.13   THE UNFINISHED STORY

This activity sparks creativity as students listen carefully, then create original conclusions to a story.

LEVEL: Intermediate—Advanced

AIM: Speaking, listening, writing

Procedure:

1. Begin telling a story. You may choose one you remember from childhood, invent one, or read one from a book.
2. Stop at a climactic point. Give students time to think of a conclusion.

Variation (speaking option):

After steps 1 and 2 above have been completed:

3. Pairs tell each other their conclusions.
4. Pairs combine into foursomes. Everyone now has the opportunity to retell their conclusion (the second time goes better) and to hear three other conclusions.
5. These groups choose one conclusion for presentation to the whole class.

Variation (writing option):

After steps 1 and 2 above have been completed:

3. Students write their conclusions.
4. Pairs read these to each other and work together on both papers to correct errors.
5. Display these on the wall for everyone to walk around and read.
6. Each student chooses one conclusion (not his or her own).
7. Volunteers read some of these aloud and the class votes to choose their favorite conclusion.

3.14 GOSSIP

This activity often leads to funny results while giving students quick feedback about their pronunciation and an immediate chance to do better.

LEVEL: Beginning—Advanced

AIM: Pronunciation, listening

Procedure:

1. Arrange students in a circle or a line.
2. Tell something short quietly into the ear of the first student. For example: "Tomorrow we're going to walk to the library and check out some books" or "Daisuke had dinner with his host family last week."

3. This student murmurs what you said to the next person, who passes it on. (If other students can overhear as the message is passed along, teach everyone to hum until their turns come.)

4. The last student tells the entire class what he or she thinks the message was. The results are usually hilarious.

5. Everyone tells their neighbor what they thought they heard. This provides speakers with useful feedback about their pronunciation.

6. Do another round immediately, encouraging everyone to speak as clearly as possible.

Note: Eight to ten students is optimal; if your group is large, demonstrate with eight to ten students, then form groups to play the game.

3.15 TWO-MINUTE PRESENTATIONS

This activity works best in small classes.

LEVEL: Intermediate—Advanced

AIM: Speaking, preview, review

MATERIALS: Timer

Procedure:

1. Assign a high-interest topic to the entire class. Possibilities:

    Decisions I Have Made
    A Problem in My Country
    A Great Problem in the World Today
    My Dream or Hope for the Future
    Why People Fight Wars
    What We Can Do to Save Our Planet
    Will There Always Be Discrimination?
    Why I Am against (or for) Capital Punishment

2. Give students five minutes to write down some ideas they have on the topic.

3. Each student gets exactly two minutes to talk about the subject in front of the class. Use a timer.

4. After everyone has spoken, students may ask questions. Class discussions often follow.

Acknowledgment: This activity is a variation of one we learned from our creative colleague Kevin Keating, who teaches at the Center for English as a Second Language (CESL) at the University of Arizona.

3.16 INTERACTION LINES

Students love this activity because they become experts on (and teachers of) their own piece of information. They also enjoy the lively interchange as everyone talks at once. Even timid students speak up!

LEVEL: Intermediate—Advanced

AIM: Review of reading material, fluency

Procedure:

1. Each student writes one good question he or she knows the answer to based on something the class has read.

2. Students stand in two rows facing each other.

3. The students in one row ask their questions, all speaking at the same time. Each partner (standing opposite) answers. (If he or she can't answer, the student who asked provides the answer.)

4. All answerers move one position to the left, so that each student faces a new partner. The student without a partner moves down the center aisle to the far position of the answerers' line. (This looks like the Virginia Reel.)

5. Each asker asks the new partner the same question. Again answerers rotate. The activity continues until they have asked their question of every student in the answerers' row.

6. Ask, "Did anyone get a particularly good answer to their question?" Askers tell the best answers they heard—e.g., "Yumiko gave me an interesting answer that I hadn't thought of . . . ."

7. The answerers now become the askers, and the activity is repeated.

Notes:

1. *This routine can be used for any questions you want your students to deal with, for example:*

   a. *questions about students' lives,*
   b. *questions about cultures,*
   c. *questions about survival skills,*
   d. *questions about any content your class is interested in.*

2. *If your class is large, create sets of rows with no more than ten in a row.*

3.17   CONTINUUMS

This activity helps students engage in meaningful discussion.

LEVEL: Intermediate—Advanced

AIM: Fluency practice, writing

Procedure:

1. Write any controversial statement on the board. It may be related to something you have been reading about. Examples:

   "Watching television is a waste of time."
   "All murderers deserve to die."
   "Women should do the cooking and cleaning."
   "Smokers are irresponsible people."
   "Lying is as bad as stealing."

2. On another place on the board, draw a horizontal line that represents a continuum. On the left end of the line, write "agree strongly;" on the right end, write "Disagree strongly."

3. Students write their names along the continuum.

4. Call on ten to fifteen students to defend their positions.

5. Students mingle and explain their positions to others.

6. In plenary, students who changed their minds explain why.

Extension (writing option): Students write about their positions.

3.18 ROLE-PLAYS

This activity brings real language needs into the classroom. It stimulates imagination and provides repeated opportunities to refine language functions.

The activity can be used for many purposes, such as previewing and reviewing readings or triggering discussions about social issues, political issues, problems students need to solve, and readings from literature.

The activity we describe here allows intermediate to advanced students to construct whole characters and create lines for those characters to say.

LEVEL: Intermediate—Advanced

AIM: Accuracy in speaking, conversation practice, vocabulary development, pronunciation

Procedure:

1. Write an example situation on the board, such as:

   A: You're in an elevator. You have severe asthma. The sign says: *No Smoking.* The elevator gets stuck. B lights up a cigarette.

   B: You are a heavy smoker. When you are nervous, you need a cigarette. You get on an elevator with a "No smoking" sign. The elevator gets stuck. You light up a cigarette. A asks you not to smoke. Defend your need for a cigarette.

2. Designate half of the class as Team A and the other half as Team B.

3. The two teams brainstorm and write down many things their characters could possibly say. This is not yet a conversation, just a list.

4. Circulate, helping students correct errors.

5. Everyone on the team practices what their character might say. They don't know yet which of them will be chosen to perform.

6. Choose an A and a B and send them to opposite corners for sixty seconds with this instruction: "Hide in the corner with your back to the class. Mutter everything you might say. Do not stop talking! Say 'Ba, ba, ba, . . .' if you need to, but keep talking."

7. While these two are muttering, arrange the rest of the class in a U shape.

8. After 60 seconds, clap your hands, signaling A and B to turn around. Still muttering and looking at the floor, they enter the middle of the U and encounter each other. Conversation spontaneously breaks out between them.

9. They finish and sit down.

10. In plenary, students tell what was good and what was useful about this first conversation. Accept one or two comments on how this presentation could be even better.

11. Choose another A and B to perform the same situation, building on what happened in the first performance and making it even better (more grammatically correct, more socially realistic, more direct eye contact, louder—whatever goals you identify).

Notes:

1. *Encourage the students to write many possible utterances during the group preparation phase. They may give their character a name and dream up a past life, family, personality, anything that may help to flesh out their character.*

   Here are two more situations you can use:

   "Bad Grades"

   A: You were lazy this term. Your grades are very low. You present your report card to your parents. Tell them why they should not be upset.

   B: Your child usually gets good grades, but he or she has just brought you a report card that is terrible! Tell your child everything a parent would say.

   "At The Doctor's"

   A: You stayed home from work because you were in a bad mood. You need a paper from a doctor excusing your absence from work. You go to Richard. He's a doctor and has been your friend for the last twenty years. He has written excuses for you many times before. Tell him what you need and why it is so important.

   B: You are Richard, a doctor. An old friend comes and asks you to write an excuse because he or she stayed home from work last week to get over a bad mood. Explain to your friend why you won't write him or her a note.

2. *Simpler role plays can be used with beginners. Students memorize dialogs from their book and practice their lines in character. In other words, they say their lines angrily, happily, sadly, emphatically, doubtfully, etc.*

Acknowledgment: We learned this activity in a workshop given by Mark Rittenberg.

3.19 CATEGORIES

People love to guess and to give clues. This association game sparks imagination and activates stored knowledge. It makes students reach a little beyond what they thought they could express in their new language.

LEVEL: Intermediate—Advanced

AIM: Fluency practice, vocabulary review and expansion

Procedure:

1. Say, "a bird, an airplane, a kite, a bee, me (in my dreams!), a balloon . . . ." Tell students the category: "Things that fly."

2. Present another set of clues: "an egg, a wine glass, someone's heart, a lightbulb (if you drop it) . . . ." Students guess the category: "Things that break!"

3. Write a new category on the board—for example, "Things that are green."

4. Each student writes examples of this category.

5. In pairs, students get their partners to guess what they've written by giving clues. For example: "This is big, and it grows outside, and you can climb in it . . . birds build nests in it . .. " until the partner guesses: "Tree!"

6. Students alternate giving clues and guessing until some finish their lists.

7. In plenary, pairs report their favorite items.

Note: Example categories:

1. *Verbs: things you can hit with, things you eat, things you can do with your feet, things you can do with your hands.*

2. *Adjectives: things that are hot or cold; or red, black or purple; or soft, hard, rough; or round, square, cubical; or sweet, sour, etc.*

Variations:

1. Write on the board two categories instead of just one. In each pair, A writes examples for one category while B does the other. Students give clues (as described in Step 5) so their partners can guess the examples they have listed.

2. To make it easier for beginners, put a category and a list of example words on the board, discuss meanings, then play the game with these words still up. For example, write on the board:

   Category: "Things that are yellow"
   Examples: the sun, the center of an egg, some flowers, a
       canary

   Students take turns giving clues about these examples.
   A: This is very big. It is hot. It is in the sky, but not at night.
   B: The sun!

Acknowledgment: We saw this activity demonstrated by our colleague at the University of Arizona, Dr. Csilla Balogh.

3.20   WHAT MACHINE AM I?

LEVEL: Intermediate—Advanced

AIM: Fluency practice, vocabulary development

Procedure:

1. List on the board all the machines and appliances students can think of.

2. Students talk about which machines are most important to them and why.

3. Each student chooses a machine that is most like himself or herself.

4. In small groups, students explain why they identify with this machine.

5. Each group chooses its most interesting explanation.

6. These chosen students form a panel and present their explanations to the class.

Extension (writing option): For homework, students write about their machines.

Variations:

1. To challenge listeners more in the small groups, you may ask a student to present a classmate's explanation.

2. Use animals instead of machines.

3.21 REAL LANGUAGE

People studying in a country where their target language is spoken are likely to encounter slang and idioms. One way to help them understand these is to set aside regular time at the beginning of class for students to ask about the strange things they have heard or seen out in the real world.

LEVEL: Intermediate—Advanced

AIM: Increasing knowledge of slang and idioms

Procedure:

1. A volunteer writes on the board a strange word or phrase he or she has found.

2. Ask if classmates can help with the meaning. Explain it yourself only if necessary.

3. Practice the new word or phrase with the whole class. Volunteers may try out new sentences using it. Chorally repeat good sentences.

4. Give everyone a moment to make notes.

5. Ask if anyone has another piece of "real language" to offer. Continue until you have a few good ones on the board.

6. Students mingle, using the new slang and idioms in sentences.

Extension:

1. Establish a class collection of "real language" that grows as the weeks go by.

2. In the final week of class, review this collection for fun. Students write the entire collection on the board, then pair up to make dialogues or stories using several "real language" items. These are performed for the class' enjoyment.

Acknowledgment: Our thanks to Dale Post, of Sahuarita Middle School in Arizona, for this idea.

Variation: To shift even more responsibility from teacher to student, you can make this a completely cooperative activity.

1. Invite students to write on the board the "real language" they want help with.

2. Students choose an item (their own or another student's) for homework. Their task is to find a native speaker or print resource, learn this new expression, and teach it to the class in a later lesson.

3.22   FOUR PICTURES MAKE A STORY

This activity sparks students' imaginations, brings about interesting conversation, and promotes vocabulary development.

LEVEL: Intermediate—Advanced

AIM: Conversation, listening, vocabulary expansion, writing practice

MATERIALS: Four interesting pictures (Any pictures will do.)

Procedure:

1. Divide your class into four groups, with at least four students in each group.

2. Give each group a picture.

3. In the groups, students look carefully at their pictures. Students describe their picture to one another thoroughly, making mental notes of as many details as possible.

4. Collect the four pictures.

5. One student (the "ambassador") leaves each group, goes to the next group, and describes his or her picture to this group. (Students in this group now have two mental pictures, one they have seen and one that has been described to them.)

6. The "ambassador" stays put. Another student from each original group moves on to repeat the process. (Each group now has three mental pictures.)

7. Repeat the process. (Each group now has four mental pictures.)

8. Each group writes a story that includes all four pictures. (A recorder writes the story as everyone contributes ideas.)

9. Each group chooses a reader to read their story aloud to the class.

10. Post the four original pictures so that the whole class can see them.

11. Ask, "Do you want to change any details in your stories?" Discuss.

Note: In large classes, use eight pictures, or twelve, or more. Keep your students in groups of four or more, but be sure to have just four groups circulate and make stories about four pictures.

Chapter Four
Reading

Researchers are constantly changing their attitudes toward reading. While some have seen it as a system of decoding, others perceive it as a "psychological guessing game," which involves all of the learner's knowledge. Getting meaning from reading in an additional language, however, is a complex skill that requires careful coaching. The activities in this chapter will actively engage students in meaningful interactions with written texts.

The first four activities highlight prereading techniques. If you have ever read a familiar old story with pleasure or chosen a newspaper article because you are familiar with that topic, you know how rewarding it can be to read when you already have a good idea about the content. Yet we often ask our students to perform the doubly challenging task of learning something new while reading in a foreign or second language. Good prereading routines help students familiarize themselves with what they will read before they tackle it. They will enjoy reading much more.

4.1   PREDICTING FROM THE TITLE

LEVEL: Beginning—Advanced
AIM: Prereading

Procedure:

1. Call students' attention to the title of a reading passage.

2. Ask them to notice other clues to what they are about to read— e.g., pictures, captions, charts, or words in bold type.

3. In small groups, students discuss what they think this reading might be about.

4. Groups report their ideas to the whole class. Note some of these on the board.

5. Students read the article.

6. In plenary, discuss how close their predictions were.

4.2   WHAT WE ALREADY KNOW

LEVEL: Beginning—Advanced
AIM: Prereading

Procedure:

1. Wake up students' background knowledge by asking, "What do we already know about _____ (the subject of their next reading)?"

2. As students offer ideas, list them on the board under three categories:

   things we know
   things we think are true
   questions we have about this subject

3. Students read the article in class or for homework. As they read, they naturally notice whether their prereading ideas are confirmed (or not confirmed!).

4. (optional) Look back at the prereading ideas after students finish reading.

4.3 TELL A TALE OF GUESSWORK

LEVEL: Intermediate—Advanced

AIM: Prereading

Procedure:

1. Tell a little about the main characters students will encounter in their next reading. For example: "This story has a poor but kind young woman, a handsome prince, a wicked stepmother, and some helpful animals." Or, if your reading is nonfiction: "This article has a large, rich country, a small country with big oil reserves, some frightened people, an army, and a happy ending."

2. Tell students they will make an imaginary story about the characters before reading. Students do one of the following options as they prepare their stories:

    a. think for one minute in silence,

    b. quick-write,

    c. write key words.

3. Choose one of these options:

    a. Students mingle, telling their one-minute stories to as many classmates as possible,

    b. Students sit in small groups. Each student tells his or her story, then the group votes on the best one (or combines elements from more than one). A spokesperson from each group tells that story in plenary.

Note: It is unimportant whether students' stories resemble the one they will read. This activity arouses their curiosity, and they approach the reading with high interest.

4.4 PRETEACHING VOCABULARY

LEVEL: Intermediate—Advanced

AIM: Prereading

Procedure:

1. Choose one of these options to introduce this activity:
   a. List on the board new words that will help your students with the reading.
   b. Have students scan for new words (a few students to each paragraph) and put them on the board.
2. Once the words are on the board, students write their names beside any word they can use in a sentence.
3. Briefly explain any words that nobody knows.
4. Students mingle, explaining the word they know to other students by using the word in a sentence. They teach the same word several times.
5. Circulate, helping students make correct sentences and offering more sentences that use the words nobody knew.
6. Students say their "vocabulary sentence" to a new partner and listen to that partner's "vocabulary sentence."
7. They move on to a new partner, saying the sentence they have just received from their previous partner.
8. This continues for several exchanges.

Extensions:

1. In plenary, ask students to write sentences using every word on the board.
   a. In larger classes, students may write their sentences on paper. Circulate to check them, and send more-advanced students around to show their good sentences to less-advanced students.
   b. For other classes, have students put these sentences on the board and then read them aloud. Make corrections when needed.
2. Choose a few of the vocabulary words and ask students to make up a story using these words. (See the previous activity, "Tell a Tale of Guesswork," for procedure.)

4.5 CLASSIC JIGSAW

An Introduction to Jigsaw Activities

The jigsaw routine is based on the information-gap strategy; students are responsible for different pieces of information and must share knowledge in order to complete an entire and comprehensive set of information. Various forms of the jigsaw can be successfully used to arouse prereading motivation as well as for review in postreading recapitulation.

The technique allows able students to become teachers and gives less-able students the opportunity to shine as experts.

LEVEL: Beginning—Advanced

AIM: Reading, speaking

Procedure:

1. Divide any text into four sections. Label these sections A, B, C, and D.

2. (optional step) Preteach difficult words.

3. Assign the different sections for silent individual reading to various students in your class. Everyone should be given one of the reading sections.

4. Students sit in groups with others who have read the same sections. A's sit with A's, B's with B's, C's with C's, and D's with D's. They talk about the content of their reading section and make notes of the most important facts. Tell them that before these groups disperse, everyone in the group must become an "expert" on their section, as it will be their job to explain this material to students who have not read it.

5. Re-group students into new "expert groups." Each group should include at least one A, one B, one C, and one D.

6. Each expert presents his or her material to the three classmates who have not read it.

7. Each expert rereads his or her piece and underlines one sentence that was especially meaningful.

8. Students tell their group which sentence they have chosen and explain why they made this choice.

9. Students return to their original group and again read and explain their sentences.

10. Students reread their passage, choosing another favorite sentence.

11. Students read their new sentence aloud and explain their choice.

12. Finish with a plenary discussion.

Note: Four is not a magic number for jigsaw activities; feel free to use two or three sections.

4.6   PARAGRAPH JIGSAW

If you haven't used a jigsaw activity before, please see page 45 for "An Introduction to Jigsaw Activities."

LEVEL: Intermediate—Advanced

AIM: Reading, speaking

Procedure:

1. Dictate the first and last sentences of the first paragraph of a new reading.

2. In small groups, students speculate on the content of the paragraph. A secretary in each group takes notes.

3. A spokesperson from each group reports to the whole class on the group's guesses.

4. Divide the class into four groups, A, B, C, and D.

5. Dictate the first and last sentences of Paragraphs 2–5, to the four groups. (You will be dictating two different sentences to each group.)

6. Each group speculates on the content of their new paragraph, each student taking notes of the main ideas as he or she listens to the people in the group. (Everyone is a "secretary" this time.)

7. Students regroup into sections that have representatives from A, B, C, and D. Each representative talks about the content decided on in his or her previous group. (If there is more than one representative from a group, they help one another to report.)

8. A spokesperson from each group reports on the group's opinion of what the entire article will be about.

   Note: This step can be very interesting because although students were given the same sentences and shared their information in the original group, the speculations of the recombined groups will be quite varied.

9. Give the entire reading passage with a summary assignment for homework or as silent reading in class.

4.7 QUESTION JIGSAW

If you haven't used a jigsaw activity before, please see page 45 for "An Introduction to Jigsaw Activities."

LEVEL: Intermediate—Advanced

AIM: Reading, speaking, pronunciation, creating questions

Procedure:

1. Divide your reading passage into four sections: A, B, C, and D.
2. Assign different reading sections to small groups of students.
3. In small groups, students read one of the sections, taking turns to read each sentence aloud.
4. In these small groups, students formulate three questions that are answered in their reading passage. A secretary writes these questions. Circulate, checking the correctness of question formation.
5. Students pass their questions on to another group. This group answers the questions, referring to their texts. A secretary writes these answers.
6. A spokesperson from each group reports the answers of the group to the entire class.
7. The class speculates on the content of the entire reading passage.
8. Assign the entire reading passage with a summary assignment for homework.

Extension: If you have enough time, students can pass the questions to the next group so that all groups will read and respond to questions about all four paragraphs.

4.8   VOCABULARY JIGSAW

If you haven't used a jigsaw activity before, please see page 45 for "An Introduction to Jigsaw Activities."

LEVEL: Intermediate—Advanced

AIM: Reading, vocabulary acquisition, speaking

Procedure:

1. Divide a reading passage into four sections: A, B, C, and D.

2. Assign one of these sections to each student in the class.

3. Students read their sections, circling words they don't know.

4. Students sit in groups with those who have read the same passage.

5. In the small groups, each student presents his or her "unknown words" and asks for explanations from fellow students. Circulate to help out.

6. Students form different groups, which have representatives from A, B, C, and D.

7. Students show each other words from their own section that they still want help with and ask for explanations.

8. Representatives from each group write the remaining "unknown words" on the board.

9. Explain the remaining words.

10. Ask students to contribute other words (those that were explained in the groups) that they think are important to the meaning of the passage. Put these words on the board.

11. In plenary, the class speculates on the content of the passage.

12. Assign reading of the passage with a summary component for home reading.

4.9 PREDICTING FROM SENTENCES

In this prereading activity students predict the content of a passage by discussing individual sentences.

LEVEL: Intermediate—Advanced

AIM: Reading, speaking

Procedure:

1. Ask each student to choose a sentence from a new text and copy it onto a slip of paper.
2. Students tape their sentences on the walls of the classroom.
3. In pairs, students walk around the room reading the sentences.
4. Students sit with their partners and reconstruct the central content of what they have read.
5. Pair joins pair and, in groups of four, students again reconstruct the content of what they have read. A secretary takes notes.
6. A spokesperson reports the ideas of each group to the class.
7. In plenary, the entire class speculates on the content of the reading passage.
8. Assign the reading passage with a summary assignment for home reading.

4.10 SCRAMBLED SENTENCES

This is an excellent, repeatable activity. Choose readings with clear coherency links between sentences.

LEVEL: Intermediate—Advanced

AIM: Reading (reordering with coherence)

MATERIALS: Blank index cards

Procedure:

1. Choose a reading students are already familiar with.
2. In plenary, number the sentences in the reading. Assign each sentence to one student. Each student copies his or her sentence onto a card.
3. Collect and mix up these cards.

4. Students put the cards back into correct order without referring to the reading. There is more than one way to do this:

   a. Students may cluster around the teacher's desk.

   b. You may line up the cards on the chalk ledge. Everyone goes up to move the cards around.

Variations (for larger classes):

1. Each group creates a set of cards and then arranges them on a desk and clusters around to reorder their set.

2. Choose a text students have not read yet. Assign different paragraphs to each group, then rotate sets of cards so that each group has to reorder a set of sentences from a paragraph they haven't read yet. When they've done their best, they may read to confirm whether they are correct.

Note: Beginning students can do this with words in a sentence. On the board, write the words of a sentence. They should be in the wrong order. Direct each student to copy one word on his or her card. Students then stand up and tell one another the words. Their goal is to stand in line with the words in the correct order to make a meaningful sentence.

4.11 STUDENT-MADE TESTS

Students review very effectively when they create their own tests.

LEVEL: Intermediate—Advanced

AIM: Reading, writing

Procedure:

1. After a unit of study, assign students to several small groups. Each group makes a test about the material. Tasks may include the following:

   a. true/false statements

   b. comprehension questions (short-answer, fill-in-the-blank, or multiple-choice)

   c. matching lists (characters with actions, characters with attributes, causes with effects, events with dates, vocabulary with definitions or synonyms)

   d. essay questions

2. Circulate, offering help and collecting usable tasks as they are finished.

3. For the test the following day, choose selected items from the groups' work. Dictate these, type them for distribution, or write them on the board.

4.12 FIND A SENTENCE

"In-reading" tasks can make the difference between students reading mechanically or reading with real interest and comprehension. This adaptable activity can be used again and again.

LEVEL: Intermediate—Advanced

AIM: Reading with a purpose, scanning, discussion, getting to know classmates, writing

Procedure:

1. Tell students, "While you are reading this, I want you to choose one sentence and write it down to share with the class." Offer the students one of the following options:

   a. a beautiful sentence
   b. a very interesting sentence
   c. a surprising sentence
   d. a sentence that contains the main idea
   e. a sentence the student doesn't understand
   f. a sentence that reminds the student of something
   g. a sentence that makes great sense to the student
   h. a sentence the student agrees or disagrees with
   i. a sentence that upsets the student

Note: Option e is particularly effective because when students slow down to identify a sentence they think they don't understand, they suddenly understand it!

2. You have choices here.

   a. Students may write their sentences on the board for class discussion.
   b. In small groups, students share their sentences, telling why they chose that sentence.

Extension (writing option):

1. Students write to expand on their own sentence or one they heard from a classmate.

2. These short compositions are posted around the walls.

3. Students circulate, reading these and writing comments at the bottom.

Variation: You may present the entire "menu" of prompts to give students more choice and/or to elicit more than one sentence from each student.

4.13   CHANGE THE FORMAT

Comprehension questions are only one way to help students understand a reading. Just as effective (and more fun for the students) is to ask them to change the format to something other than prose, using information they have read. Students activate their best reading strategies because they aren't just answering questions for a teacher who already knows the answers anyway. Instead, they're using what they've read to produce something.

LEVEL: Intermediate—Advanced

AIM: Reading comprehension

Procedure:

Choose a text students have read. It may be fiction or nonfiction. Ask them to change the information from prose to something else. Some options you may suggest include:

1. a time line of the events

2. a picture of an event or scene from the reading

3. a chart or graph of the information

4. a poem, song, jazz chant, or rap based on what they read

5. a dialog that could have occurred between two or more of the characters

Note: Reversing the direction works just as well. For example, students might:

1. *look at a bus schedule, then write a narrative about someone's adventures traveling;*

2. *read a menu and write an account of someone's delicious (or disgusting, or unusual) meal;*

3. *read a chart and write an analysis of the issue/problem.*

4.14 TELLING BACK AND FORTH

This activity challenges students to read carefully, paraphrase, and listen carefully. The feedback students give each other at each step clarifies the meaning of what they have read and heard.

LEVEL: Intermediate—Advanced

AIM: Reading, speaking, writing

Procedure:

1. Choose two short texts. These can be unrelated or they can be, for example, Paragraph 1 and Paragraph 2 (or the first and last paragraphs) of a reading.

2. Put students in pairs.

3. Every A student reads the first text; every B student reads the other text.

4. The A's put their text away, then tell the B's all about what they just read.

5. Then each B tells A everything he or she just heard A say.

6. A repeats information if B misunderstood or forgot something important.

7. B retells what he or she has heard until A is satisfied.

8. Then both students look at A's text to discover together whether A's telling was complete and correct.

9. Follow the same procedure for the text the B's have.

Extension (writing option): Students put away the texts again and write in their own words what they have understood of both texts. They exchange these paraphrases with someone other than their original partners for oral or written feedback.

Note: Consider using jokes for this activity.

4.15   READING WITH HALF THE WORDS

Most students become anxious if they find words they don't know in a reading. This activity demonstrates how much they can understand after reading only 50 percent of the words.

LEVEL: Intermediate—Advanced

AIM: Building confidence in reading ability

Procedure:

1. Choose a short, relatively easy reading passage from the students' book.

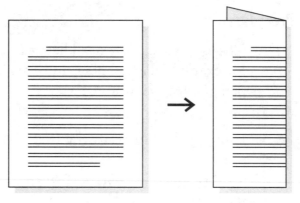

2. In class, students fold this page in half from top to bottom. Students can see only the left half of the text.

3. Give them time to read it.

4. In plenary, ask students what they understood. Useful prompts:

    a. Yes/no questions, e.g.: "Was this about astronomy?" ("No! It's about farming in Africa.") "Does this story have a sad ending? ("No, he got a lot of money.")

    b. Short-answer questions, e.g.: "What is the big problem?" ("There isn't enough water for the farms.") "How many people are in this story?" ("Three: Jack, his mother, and a giant.")

    c. Open-ended questions, e.g., "What else?" "Tell me one more thing."

5. When the class has collectively recalled/guessed as much as they can, congratulate them! Point out that if they can understand so much after reading only half the words, maybe understanding every word is not very important after all. Ask if they are willing to:

a. try reading without using their dictionaries so often,

b. read fast sometimes, even if they don't understand everything, and

c. read easy things in the target language without stopping, just for fun.

Tell them that researchers have discovered that reading a lot will help them improve their language skills fast!

4.16 OVERHEAD SUMMARIES

Summarizing activates students' best reading strategies. This activity provides peer support.

LEVEL: Intermediate—Advanced

AIM: Reading, summarizing, speaking

MATERIALS: Overhead projector, transparencies, markers (See number 2 under variations if you don't have these.)

Procedure:

1. Divide a long reading into sections.

2. Assign each section to a small group of students. (Groups of three work best.)

3. Each group appoints a secretary and two spokespersons.

4. Students silently read the passages assigned to them.

5. Each group summarizes their passage.

6. The secretaries write the main points of the passages on the transparencies.

7. The spokespersons come to the front of the class and explain their summaries to the rest of the class.

8. When all summaries have been presented, the entire passage is reviewed by the class.

Variations:

1. You can assign the individual readings and summaries as homework. In class, students sit with classmates who have done the same reading. They compare their summaries and make a group summary, which is presented to the class on transparencies.

2. If you don't have transparencies (and if your class is small enough), groups can produce their summaries at the board.

4.17   Quick-Skim

This activity encourages readers to take risks and read faster. It is game-like and communal, so that even though students are doing something that is quite challenging, anxiety doesn't creep in.

LEVEL: Beginning—Advanced

AIM: Increasing students' reading speed

Procedure:

1. Tell students, "Sometimes we read to understand completely. But other times we look at a reading to decide whether it is interesting enough to read. Or we look at a reading to get a quick, general idea about it. Let's practice taking a quick look at a reading."

2. Choose a page from the students' book.

3. Demonstrate "finger drag" to carry eyes down the page by holding your book up for all to see, positioning your finger in the middle of the first line of text, and moving your finger straight down the middle of the text for fifteen seconds. (A student can time you.) Then close your book.

4. Tell students, "I didn't look at all the words. I looked only at the middle of the page. My eyes followed my fingers. But I can remember some things!" Tell them several words you saw. Keep this very simple, so they don't feel pressured by your example.

5. Students open their books to a different reading.

6. When you call, "Begin!," students do a "finger drag" down the page. Call, "Stop!" after fifteen seconds.

7. In plenary, students pool their knowledge, recalling everything they can. It usually surprises them that they caught not just single words (as you did, in your demonstration) but whole phrases and even general ideas. If they are collectively getting about half the meaning, you have found the right level. If not, adjust the length or the difficulty level of the passage next time.

Note: Eventually, students realize that skimming is not only a game, but a very useful technique that they can apply to many reading tasks.

Acknowledgment: We wish to thank Laurel's sister, Darcie Smith, a creative elementary-school teacher in Nevada, for this useful activity.

Chapter Five
Writing

Writing is generally considered the most difficult of the four skills. It demands a great deal of work and concentration. On the other hand, writing brings students a great sense of pride as they produce pieces of their own creation. Writing helps us to organize our thoughts. It is the skill that shows how well we control language.

What shall we do when we want to make writing an active process with peer input, but some students show up without their written assignments? Our advice is to have those students work hard at improving the work of classmates and/or do their own writing in class. Mean-

while, students who come prepared receive a lot of helpful feedback from their teacher and from peers. Students who once experience the "outcast position" might just not want to repeat it!

Writing is not just challenging for students. It is also challenging and time-consuming for the teacher. With the well-designed activities in this chapter, students receive plenty of opportunities to write and to receive feedback for improvement while you reduce the time you spend in preparation and paper-grading.

5.1 THREE UNRELATED THINGS

LEVEL: Intermediate—Advanced

AIM: Writing, speaking

Procedure:

1. In plenary, ask students for the names of three things that have no relationship to each other. For example, students might suggest a snake, a piece of dirty paper, and a rainbow. Write these on the board.

2. Tell students that they will write or tell a creative story that includes all three things. Give students one full minute to think about their story.

3. Students write their stories.

4. Pairs read these to each other and work together on both papers to correct errors.

5. Display these on the wall for everyone to walk around and read.

6. Each student chooses one story (not his or her own).

7. Volunteers read some of these aloud and the class votes for their favorite story.

Extension (speaking option): Instead of writing, you may want students to just tell their stories.

1. Follow Steps 1 and 2.

2. Pairs tell each other their stories.

3. Pairs combine into foursomes. Everyone now retells his or her own story (this second telling goes better) and hears three other stories.

4. Groups choose one story for presentation to the whole class.

5.2 THE CLASSIC DICTACOMP

An Introduction to Dictacomps

The "Dictacomp" is a combination of two techniques—dictation and composition. It is an excellent way to teach paraphrasing. A highly adaptable routine, dictacomp can also be used for pre-reading, reviewing material, recycling vocabulary, and reinforcing a grammar point. The great advantage of a dictacomp is that it provides instant feedback.

Dictacomps are adaptable. Depending on your purposes, students may try to reconstruct the original precisely, or they may paraphrase, using prompts to recreate meaning in their own words.

LEVEL: Beginning—Advanced

AIM: Writing, paraphrasing, listening

Procedure:

1. Choose any short reading passage from the students' text—no longer than a paragraph.

2. Write several of the key vocabulary items on the board.

3. Together with students, clarify the meanings of the chosen words.

4. Read the passage aloud slowly. Students have their books closed.

5. Read the passage again at a normal pace.

6. Students write the passage trying to get it as close as possible to the original.

7. In pairs, students compare their papers, adding or correcting as needed.

8. Students open their books to check on both content and language aspects of their passage.

9. Volunteers read their final versions aloud.

10. In plenary, the class talks about the most difficult aspects of the exercise.

5.3 STUDENT-TO STUDENT DICTACOMP

This activity lets students help each other to reproduce meaning and to focus on accuracy.

LEVEL: Beginning—Advanced

AIM: Writing, spelling, structure, punctuation, pronunciation

MATERIALS: A dictionary

Procedure:

1. In pairs, students choose a passage they want to work on.
2. These pairs read their passage to each other, taking turns reading one sentence each, aloud.
3. Students reread the passage silently, circling words they don't understand.
4. Students mingle, asking each other and you about the meanings of words they don't understand. They may also use the dictionary, which should be readily available on your desk.
5. As soon as the vocabulary has been clarified, students sit in pairs, facing their original partners.
6. Students divide their reading passage into two sections.
7. Student A reads his or her section while Student B listens with book closed.
8. Student B reads his or her section while Student A listens with book closed.
9. They repeat Steps 7 and 8 at a faster pace.
10. With books closed, both students write out their sections as close to the original as possible.
11. With open books, students check each other's papers for correctness of language and content.
12. Students return their partners' papers and review the corrections.
13. With books closed, the pair re-creates the whole passage (both sections). Both may talk while one writes, or they may take turns writing. This step produces one paper.
14. With books open, students check what they have done a final time.

Extension: Some pairs tell their passages to the entire class. They don't read from their papers; rather, they recount the passage with their papers turned down. They may glance at the papers a few times, if necessary.

Variation: Students can write the section they have listened to rather than the one they have read aloud.

5.4 GROUP-TO-GROUP DICTACOMP

This activity is particularly useful in a content-based course and can be used as both review and preview.

Save this activity for a day when you have plenty of time for your students to reconstruct a reading. While they settle in to work on Step 13, you have time to do other things.

LEVEL: Intermediate—Advanced

AIM: Writing, listening, vocabulary

Procedure:

1. Divide a reading passage into four sections, A, B, C, and D.
2. Divide your class into four groups and assign each group one of the sections. (In large classes, divide your class into eight or more groups and assign the same section to two or more groups.)
3. In the groups, students read their passage aloud, taking turns reading one sentence at a time.
4. Students circle the words they did not understand and help each other with meanings. Circulate, helping as needed.
5. In each group, students choose a reader. The reader reads the entire passage aloud while others listen with their books closed.
6. Students choose a second reader, and the procedure is repeated.
7. With their books closed, students write out their passage as close to the original as they can recall.
8. With their books still closed, students compare their work.
9. With their books open, students check what they have written for accuracy and content.
10. Students send a messenger to another group to become the reader of their passage to that group.

11. Messengers perform a dictacomp in the new groups:
    a. They read their passage aloud twice.
    b. The three listeners reproduce the passage on paper.
    c. With the reader, the group checks all three papers for accuracy and content.

12. The procedure is repeated, with the same messengers circulating to all groups. (The messengers' pronunciation improves with feedback.)

13. With their books closed, students write out the entire reading (all four sections) as well as they can recall it.

14. Students check their work against the text.

15. Students mingle, telling each other about one fact that made an impression on them in the passage they have re-created.

5.5 ACTING-OUT DICTACOMP

This activity wakes up a class and is particularly useful in beginning classes that enjoy Total Physical Response (TPR) or with writing passages that involve a procedure.

LEVEL: Beginning—Advanced
AIM: Writing

Procedure:

1. Choose from the students' text a reading passage that involves a series of actions.

    Examples: getting up in the morning, starting a car, getting on an airplane, hunting, taking a test, preparing a meal, finding an apartment

2. With students' books closed, read the passage aloud slowly.

3. Elicit key words from the class and put these on the board.

4. Reread the passage at normal speed.

5. Mime the passage, as students write down each of your actions.

6. One volunteer at a time acts out the passage as other students call out the actions.

7. Students check their writing against the text.

Extension: Students create their own short "action passages" and in small groups act these out while fellow students write out what is being enacted.

5.6 MISSING WORDS DICTACOMP

This activity is good for recycling vocabulary. It also works well as a pre-reading activity.

LEVEL: Intermediate—Advanced

AIM: Writing, listening

Procedure:

1. From your students' textbook, choose any new paragraph that is not too long or too hard.

2. Students keep their books closed as you read the paragraph three times. Increase speed with each reading, but do not exceed normal speed.

3. Reread the paragraph a fourth time. This time leave out about five to ten key words. Make a sound such as "mmmm" in place of each missing word.

4. When you make the "mmmm" sound, students write the word they think you left out.

5. In small groups, students pool their lists of missing words.

6. Individually, students write the passage as well as they can remember it, using as prompts the missing words they wrote.

7. In small groups, students compare what they have written.

8. Each group appoints a secretary. They rewrite the passage as a group effort.

9. A reader from each group reads the group's passage. The class compares and evaluates these for correctness of language and content.

Note: Accept paraphrasing and synonyms; meaning is what's important here.

5.7 SENTENCE-BY-SENTENCE DICTACOMP

This dictacomp demands a certain logic that appeals to students who are fond of cognitive reasoning.

LEVEL: Intermediate—Advanced

AIM: Writing

Procedure:

1. Assign one sentence from a new reading to each student. (Don't use more than about two paragraphs of text.) In large classes, give the same sentence to several students.

   One good way to assign sentences is to say, "What is the first word of Sentence 1?" Students call it out. Say, "That's yours, Ahmed." Continue to assign the other sentences.

2. Students memorize their sentences and put away their texts.

3. Students write their sentences on the board. Sentence order is not important.

   Note: In large classes, students sit in small groups and write their sentences on one central piece of paper. Each group has the full collection of sentences.

4. One at a time, students read their own sentences from the board or the piece of paper.

5. Everyone reads a sentence that is not his or her own.

6. Everyone reads another new sentence, again not his or her own.

7. Everyone memorizes a new sentence.

8. Everyone recites his or her new sentence to a partner.

9. In small groups, students tell each other the content of the entire passage. (Even though the sentences are all jumbled on the board or the piece of paper, the meaning of the passage comes through!)

10. Erase all the sentences from the board. (In large classes, take away the paper from each group.)

11. Individually, students write out the entire passage.

12. In small groups, students compare passages, making additions and corrections as needed.

13. Students check their passages with the original, making corrections for language and content.

5.8 REVISION: I CAN DO IT MYSELF!

This routine saves the composition teacher a great deal of time by strengthening students' "monitors." They learn to correct "old" errors before handing in any new piece of writing. The teacher is thus free to concentrate on helping students identify their next steps in improving their writing.

LEVEL: Beginning—Advanced

AIM: Improving students' ability to edit their own work

Procedure:

1. If possible, have every student buy a simple two-pocket folder. This will hold formal compositions but no other work.

2. Write on the board in big, block letters these two sentences: Things I already know and will always do correctly.

   If I checked all these things, I am ready to give my composition to my teacher.

   Every student writes the first sentence at the top and the second sentence at the bottom of a clean piece of paper:

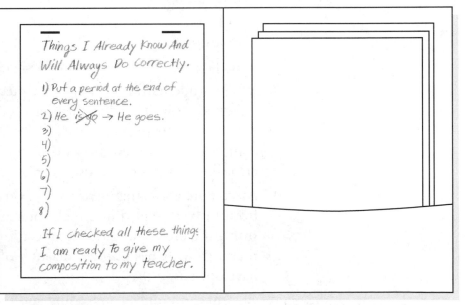

3. Pass around a stapler. As students write their names on the outside of their folders and staple the paper on the left inside, explain how the folders will be used.

4. Ask students what they all can do correctly in their compositions. To help them get started, mention such things as centering

a title at the top of the page, indenting paragraphs, making sure subjects and verbs agree, or using a spelling checker. Write your ideas and students' ideas on the board.

5. Students write the number 1 on the paper you gave them and copy from the list on the board something they know they can always do correctly. They continue listing more things, with each student including only what he or she is sure they will never do incorrectly in a paper they hand in.

6. These papers remain in the folder throughout your course, along with successive drafts of assigned compositions. Each time a student masters something, offer congratulations and ask whether he or she wants to add it to their list (perhaps with an example). It is important that students, not you, choose what goes on their lists.

7. Before students hand in each composition, give them class time to use their lists in editing their work. Encourage them to look for only one thing at a time. This will take some modeling and persistence until students notice for themselves how many errors they miss when they read their work globally. (Peers can help.)

8. While this is going on, write on the board:

    "Do I have any questions to ask my teacher before I hand in this composition?"

    Circulate, taking advantage of these "teachable moments."

9. When students finally hand in a piece of writing, they are, in effect, assuring you that they have taken responsibility for the errors on their personal lists. Sometimes it is possible to scan compositions as they are handed in. If a student has missed an error listed on his or her list, don't accept the composition.

10. As you are correcting their work, you have each student's list in front of you, stapled into their folder. It takes very little time to scan it before reading the composition. If you do find an error that a student has claimed mastery of but did not correct, you have options.

     a. You can simply stop reading and return that paper to the student.

     b. You may (or may not) automatically adjust the grade. This sounds harsh but quickly sets a new standard for students who have been lazy about applying what they know.

c. If a student is usually conscientious but somehow missed one error, you may decide to write in the margin the number from the student's list that corresponds to that error, perhaps adding a ! or a friendly "oops!" Conscientious students are chagrined and pay particular attention to that error next time.

You will know best how to handle this with your own students, but remember that keeping the standards high will pay off in a considerable reduction of the time you spend grading papers. At the same time, students will be proud of their work and of themselves.

Note: Accumulating all drafts for all compositions in a special folder provides students (and you) with proof that they are continually leaving old errors behind and mastering new ways to improve their writing. This is very satisfying. Even advanced students, who can become jaded when their language development seems to have reached a "plateau," often respond to this routine with renewed motivation to write better.

5.9 PEER REVISION I: WHAT I THINK YOU SAID

Focusing not on editorial details but on meaning, this global routine for peer review quickly leads students into work on clarity and completeness of expression. A side benefit is that pronunciation improves as author/readers struggle to make themselves understood.

LEVEL: Intermediate—Advanced

AIM: Peer revision of compositions, listening, paraphrasing, pronunciation

Procedure:

1. Students have produced a piece of writing, for homework or in class.

2. In pairs, students take turns reading their work to their partners. The reading should be done slowly. During this reading, the reader stops periodically and says, "What did I say?"

   Note: The pauses can be after one or two sentences (for beginners), after each paragraph, or after a whole composition (for very advanced students). Demonstrate, showing that the passages must be long enough so that listeners can't use short-term memory to parrot back what they heard, but must understand, and then retell in their own words, a "chunk" of meaning.

3. The listener paraphrases what he or she has understood.

4. The author/reader responds. Put a few model responses up on the board, such as:

   "Yes, that's right!"

   "Yes, but you forgot something: I also said . . . ."

   "Partly correct. Here's what I really meant: . . . ."

   "No, that's not what I tried to say. Let me explain."

5. Often, what the author/reader says is clearer than what he or she wrote! Together, the pair discusses what changes in the writing will make the meaning more clear.

Note: The author/reader, of course, is the final judge of what to change.

5.10 PEER REVISION II: EDITING WRITTEN WORK IN PAIRS

When students help one another by editing their written work together, it is clear that the editing student is helping the writer. The hidden benefit—which soon becomes clear to students—is that their own written work begins to have fewer errors. The detachment of working on someone else's paper allows them to notice errors more easily; after a time, they begin spotting more errors in their own writing.

LEVEL: Beginning—Advanced

AIM: Correcting compositions

Procedure:

1. Write on the board a list of things to look for in peer editing. Students copy this as you write. Here are some ideas you might include. You will, of course, know what you want your own students to focus on.

   Note: It is impossible to focus effectively on more than one idea at a time. Tell students to reread the compositions they edit several times, each time focusing on just one item from the list.

Revision:
1. Is my composition interesting?
2. Is it easy for my reader to understand?
3. Did I organize my ideas clearly?
4. Did I provide enough supporting details?
5. Is each paragraph clearly about one central idea?
6. Do I have a good introduction?
7. Do I have a good conclusion?

Editing:
8. Did I write a title?
9. Did I capitalize important words in the title?
10. Did I indent every paragraph?
11. Does every sentence have a capital letter and a period or other punctuation?
12. Did I check every verb to be sure I used correct forms?
    singular / plural
    tense
13. (Add other things you want your students to focus on.)

2. In pairs, students review first one composition, then the other, before handing them in to you. It is important to use words like *help* and *improve* in your instructions, rather than *look for errors* or *correct*. For example, say: "Let's make sure this is our best work. I'll give you some time to help each other improve your work before you hand it in."

3. As the pairs work, circulate and continue to use this positive language. Some students are reluctant to point out *errors* for fear of being rude, and nobody likes to feel criticized. They are much more willing to give and receive *help*.

Note: This routine can be used in conjunction with "Revision: I Can Do It Myself!" in this chapter (page 65). Students can review their personal lists and also give help to peers before handing in their work.

Variation: It's useful to focus on just one error sometimes, instead of using the whole list. Perhaps your students have done a "quick-write," for example. (See the following activity.) You might put on the board only one thing:

"Did I avoid run-on sentences by punctuating my sentences correctly?"

Students pair up to locate subjects and verbs and make decisions about where to put punctuation.

5.11   QUICK-WRITE

This activity stimulates imagination and helps students leap beyond the barrier of writer's block.

LEVEL: Intermediate—Advanced

AIM: Fluent writing

Procedure:

1. Tell students, "You will have five minutes. Fill up a paper with as many sentences as possible. It's OK if you make a lot of mistakes. If you can't think of a word you need, leave a blank space or put in a word from another language. If you don't have any ideas, keep your pen moving like this (draw a spiral on the board) until your next idea comes to you. The only rule is: *Don't stop writing! Keep your pen moving!*"

Until the end of the day. llllll llll llllllllllllllll lllllllll llllllll and then they . . .

2. Dictate an unfinished sentence. This might be related to a reading or discussion, or to the students' lives, or to a composition they will be writing soon. For fun, have students propose their own high-interest topics sometimes. Some topics that have set our students on fire are:

When I remember my school days . . .
When I think of vacations, I . . .
I'll never forget the time I lost . . .
Sometimes you just have to tell a lie because . . .
I just hate it when people . . .
The person I admire most is . . .
I get very upset when . . .
I really needed help when . . .
The best present I ever gave someone was . . .
The best present I ever got was . . .
I feel frightened when . . .
I felt like a real success when . . .
A dream that I have for my country is . . .
The most serious problem in the world today is . . .
The best way to cure a cold is . . .

3. While students are writing, it's best to keep your distance. Circulating among them may reawaken their nervousness about making mistakes. If anyone stops writing for more than ten seconds, catch that student's eye and point to the spiral on the board. They should keep their pen moving.

4. When the five minutes are up, invite students to hold up their papers to display how much they have written. Congratulate them!

5. Ask students what is good about this activity. Accept all their answers and be sure to bring up the point that we don't need to have ideas all complete in our minds before we write. Writing fast is one way to discover ideas.

6. Options for follow-up activities include the following:
    a. Students read these papers to each other in pairs.
    b. Students edit their papers for one kind of error (for example, run-on sentences or correct verb forms).
    c. Students take the papers home and develop them into the first draft of a composition.

Notes:

1. *Sometimes, you will simply end the activity after Step 5. Students are left with the satisfaction of having produced a large amount of writing in a short amount of time.*

2. *Quick-writes can be shorter than five minutes. They are wonderful fillers at the beginning or end of class.*

5.12 COUNTRIES, STATES, AND CITIES

This activity is particularly interesting in a multicultural class. Incidentally, students learn how to spell many place names.

LEVEL: Intermediate—Advanced

AIM: Writing, reading, speaking

Procedure:

1. Students sit in a circle.
2. Appoint a secretary who will record responses on the board.
3. Say the name of any city or country. Example: New York.
4. The student on your right says the name of a city, state, or country that begins with either the last or the next-to-last letter in the city you have said. Example: "Kansas" or "Rio de Janeiro."
5. Students who can't think of a response are allowed to say, "Pass."
6. The chain continues until interest lags.
7. Students choose one of the places written on the board and write a one-paragraph description of the place without mentioning it by name.
8. Students post their descriptions around the walls of the room.
9. Students walk about the room reading the descriptions. On the posted papers, they write the names of the places they think are described.
10. Students take their own papers off the walls. They give their paragraphs a title that includes the name of the place described.
11. Students read their descriptions aloud.
12. After each paper is read, students who thought the description referred to a different place explain why they thought so.

Note: Students naturally choose names of places they know, so this activity often leads to interesting cross-cultural exchanges.

5.13 REMEMBER THE PICTURE

This activity generates interesting sentences and touches students' competitive spirit.

LEVEL: Intermediate—Advanced

AIM: Writing

MATERIALS: Any interesting picture, timer

Procedure:

1. Divide your class into groups of four or five students each. Each group gives itself a name.

2. Ask the class, "What is a sentence?" Elicit their ideas and write a useful working definition on the board. For example:

   "A sentence is a group of words that
   make sense together,
   are a complete thought, and
   have a subject and a predicate."

3. Show an interesting picture, preferably one with many details. Say, "Try to remember everything in this picture," and make sure that everyone gets a good look. Then put the picture away.

4. In their groups, students generate as many sentences as they can about the picture. Ask them to refer to the definition of a sentence and say, "Only complete and correct sentences will win points for your team." A recorder writes sentences as the group generates them. (Give them five minutes; use the timer.)

5. Ask how many sentences each group has.

6. All recorders go to the board to write the sentences their group has produced.

7. While this is happening, each group is assigned to watch a recorder who is not their own. Their task is to spot incorrect or faulty sentences.

8. Circulate, confirming when a sentence is not acceptable. These are erased; only sentences that are grammatically and factually correct stay up on the board.

9. The group whose recorder has the most correct sentences on the board is the winner.

10. In plenary, show the picture again. Students notice what they had forgotten about it and generate more sentences.

5.14 WRITTEN ARGUMENT

This activity generates a lot of laughter as students write. What makes this activity particularly interesting is that students are forced to see both sides of an issue.

LEVEL: Intermediate—Advanced

AIM: Writing

Procedure:

1. Students sit in a circle. Each student has some paper and a pen.

2. Tell them the following story, perhaps adjusting language level for some classes:

   "You are the roommate of someone who never cleans the room that the two of you live in. Your roommate is a brilliant student who keeps promising you that she will do her share in cleaning, but somehow she always forgets. It is true that she frequently edits your papers and helps you with a good phrase or an idea, and this is why, most of the time, you have forgiven her for not cleaning.

   However, this time things have gone too far. You had to go away for the weekend and your roommate promised you that she would clean the room. Now it is Monday morning. You have just returned and you have to rush to class. When you walk into the room, you see a horrendous mess: papers all over, leftover food on the desk, beds unmade, dust everywhere. The place stinks! As you stand there, the door opens and your roommate walks in."

   Say, "Please write the first thing you would say."

3. Students write for a few minutes. When you see most of them looking up, say, "Please finish the sentence you are writing. Do not begin a new sentence."

4. Everyone passes their papers to the right.

5. Students read what the person on their left has written and they write an answer as the roommate who didn't clean.

6. When you tell them it is time, students pass their papers back to the left. They now write as the original angry roommate. (Each student is corresponding with two neighboring students and, as a result, is assuming two different roles.)

7. Continue the procedure as long as students seem very engaged and interested (usually half an hour).

8. Students take home their dialogues to expand, add, and improve.

Note: You can, of course, use this technique for any kind of argument-related topic or situation. For example:

   a. *generating ideas for a student's real problem (Perhaps Daisuke has to go downtown to contest a speeding ticket tomorrow, or Maria needs her deposit back from her reluctant landlord.)*

   b. *creating a dialogue two angry characters from a story, movie, or TV program, might say*

   c. *preparing for a debate by arguing two sides of a controversial topic*

Extension: Options for the following day include:

1. Students exchange, read, and correct one another's dialogues.

2. Students pair up to act out their dialogues, with praise and suggestions from the class after each performance.

Acknowledgment: This is a variation of an activity we learned from Mario Rinvolucri during an IATEFL (International Association for the Teaching of English as a Foreign Language) conference.

5.15 GIFT EXCHANGE

This vocabulary-enriching activity helps to build a pleasant and supportive classroom climate. It is as much fun for students as giving and receiving real presents. You might use this activity when a student in your class has a birthday or at the end of a course.

LEVEL: Advanced Beginning—Intermediate

AIM: Writing, speaking

MATERIALS: Small box

Procedure:

1. To make sure that everyone gets presents, have every student put his or her name on a slip of paper and drop it into the box. Students choose a name at random each time they're ready to give another present.

2. Together with the class, create a list on the board of what people like to give and receive as presents.

3. On the board write the following formulas.

Dear _____,
I would like to give you _____ for
a present because _____.

        Yours,

        _____

Dear _____,
Thanks so much for _____. It
was _____

_____ .

        Sincerely,

        _____

4. Students pick anyone in class and get busy sending that person a "present." That is, everyone creates a "present" note.

5. When a student finishes his or her "present" note, he or she folds it, delivers it to the recipient, and returns to his or her desk to write either a thank-you note or another "present" note.

6. Each time students receive a "present" note, they immediately write and deliver a thank-you note.

7. The writing can continue for about half an hour as students busily rush about and happily "open their presents."

8. Students talk to the whole class about their favorite "presents."

5.16   WHO IS THIS?

This activity encourages students to notice detail, to make their written language clear and specific, and to give feedback. It also gives every student a bit of personal attention.

LEVEL: Intermediate—Advanced

AIM: Writing, listening, recycling vocabulary

Procedure:

1. Students look around the class and write a half-page positive description of a classmate. Encourage them to be as detailed as possible. (Give a fifteen-minute time limit for this phase.)

2. In pairs, students read their descriptions aloud to each other. Tell listeners to hear the entire description. Listeners identify the student described and tell which detail in the description was most revealing.

3. Students post their descriptions around the room. Everyone walks around, reading these and writing comments. Instruct them to write only positive comments. For example: "I like Rasheed's new haircut, too." "Don't forget to mention her beautiful eyes!"

4. The class votes on the best description. (They are not allowed to vote for their own.)

5. The writer of this description reads it to the entire class.

5.17   BUDDY JOURNALS

In this activity, students are active and productive while the teacher has half an hour to give individual attention to those who need it.

LEVEL: Intermediate—Advanced

AIM: Free writing, getting to know one another, reading

MATERIALS: Small box

Procedure:

1. Early in your course, ask students to provide notebooks for journals and to write their names in them. Collect these.

2. At the beginning of the course, dictate a set of topics; one student will write each topic on a slip of paper, show it to you, and drop it into the box. Possible topics:

Foods I Love
A Favorite Vacation
What I Want in a Good Friend
Something I Am Proud Of
A Book I Loved
A Film I Loved
Why I Hate Dentists
The Way I Feel about Money
My Ideal House
A Decision I Had to Make
My Favorite Relative

3. At the beginning of each week, assign new partners for buddy journals.

4. Assign a day on which journals are to be written in class.

5. On the assigned day, give half an hour to journal writing.

6. Students choose a slip from the "topic box." If they don't like the topic, they may return it and pick another. If neither topic suits them, they may write about any topic they themselves choose. They have fifteen minutes to write.

7. Students exchange journals with journal buddies.

They have fifteen minutes to respond and react in writing to what their partner has written.

Notes:

1. *Some students ask to keep the same buddy for several weeks. If they do, let them, but having the weekly partner switch as an option saves those students who really do not enjoy one partner or who want to get to know several classmates.*

2. *Offering the "topic box" works well because when told, "Write about anything," students may feel overwhelmed and be unable to decide.*

5.18 CLOZE DICTATION

This writing activity promotes attention to detail and student self-correction.

LEVEL: Beginning—Advanced

AIM: Writing, spelling, vocabulary development, content review

Procedure:

1. Choose a passage students have already read. It should not be longer than two paragraphs—much shorter for beginning classes.

2. In pairs, students create two different cloze passages by rewriting the paragraphs they have been given, putting in blank spaces for each word they leave out. (They should leave out one word every seven to ten words.) In each of their passages different words should be left out.

3. Each pair passes their two cloze passages to another pair.

4. In pairs, students dictate to each other the passages they just received. When they are finished they should both have the original paragraph.

5. Students check their work with the original.

Acknowledgment: This is a no-preparation variation of an activity we learned in a workshop from Mario Rinvolucri.

5.19 ONE-MINUTE FEEDBACK

Why wait for the end of the course to find out from our students what they are learning? This activity gives us valuable feedback about what our students got (and didn't get) from a lesson. At the same time, it reinforces for the students what they have learned, giving them a feeling of satisfaction.

LEVEL: Intermediate—Advanced

AIM: Writing practice, feedback for teacher about what students are learning

MATERIALS: Blank index cards

Procedure:

1. When students come into class, hand each a card. Tell them that at the end of class you will ask them to write on the card what they learned today and give the card to you.

2. Be sure they put their cards away.

3. Allow one minute at the end of class for each student to write his or her note to you. Because the time is so short, students are concise, and you need only a few minutes after class to read their notes and incorporate what they have said into your planning.

Notes:

1. *Once students are accustomed to this, once they have come to expect to write you this note, they become more aware during the class of what they are and are not learning. This leads to increased student responsibility for their learning and more questions during class.*

2. *In conjunction with "One-Minute Feedback," let students determine the pace of the class by asking such questions as, "Are you ready to move on?" "Do you need more time with this?" "Should we practice this some more, or is this enough?" When we remember to do this, our classes stay in that exciting "challenge zone" where students are neither bored nor overwhelmed.*

5.20 FACES

This activity stimulates imagination, leads to interesting conversations, and makes students realize how quickly we make up our minds about people.

LEVEL: Intermediate—Advanced

AIM: Writing, speaking, vocabulary expansion

MATERIALS: A stack of magazines, paper clips

Procedure:

1. Students look through magazines to find pictures of people. (Ask them to find close-ups of faces if they can.)

2. Students tear out the pictures. Spread these out in a central place (perhaps your desk, a table, or the floor).

3. Each student chooses a picture someone else found.

4. Each student takes out a piece of paper.

5. Students sit in groups of five.

6. Dictate the following sentences:

   "My name is _____."

   "I live in _____ with _____."

7. Students write these sentences on their papers, complete them, and attach the paper to their picture with a paper clip.

8. Students pass the paper with the picture to the person on their right.

9. Students read what is on the paper they received and study the picture.

10. Dictate: "Recently, I have been very happy because _____."

11. Repeat Steps 7 and 8 (They clip and pass the paper and picture.)

12. Dictate: "I used to _____, but now I _____."

13. Students clip and pass again.

14. Dictate: "I have changed my mind about _____."

15. Students clip and pass again.

16. Dictate: "Today is my birthday. All I really want is _____."

17. Students clip and pass again.

18. At this stage, each picture has returned to the person who started it.

19. In their groups, students read their stories aloud.

20. Each group chooses their favorite story to be read in front of the class.

21. In plenary, the class talks about how and why they made up their minds about the people in the pictures. This usually leads to interesting discussions of stereotypes and first impressions.

Chapter Six
Vocabulary

To the average learner, learning a new language means learning words, words, and more words. While this attitude may seem simplistic, it is not without its merit. The knowledge of words, as any traveler to foreign lands knows, is crucial in early communication and empowering in later use of language. Our students are constantly meeting new words in new contexts. They need time and opportunity to consolidate their knowledge as they practice and use their new-found friends. The activities in this chapter offer interesting and meaningful ways to encounter, store, and recycle vocabulary.

6.1 FROM COLD TO HOT

This activity expands vocabulary domains, helping students to understand the great variety of expression in the language they are studying.

LEVEL: Intermediate—Advanced

AIM: Vocabulary expansion and practice

MATERIALS: A thesaurus

Procedure:

1. Together with your class, compose a list of words that mean *cold*. You might come up with *chilly, cold, frosty, icy, wintry, freezing*.

2. A volunteer looks up *cold* in the thesaurus to find more words and dictates these to you as you write them on the board. Discuss meanings as the words go up on the board.

3. Repeat the procedure with the word *hot*. You might come up with *lukewarm, fiery, heated, sultry, sweltering* and *scalding*.

4. A new volunteer checks *hot* in the thesaurus for more contributions, and you write these on the board. Again, discuss meanings as the words go up on the board.

5. Each student chooses one word from the board. They line up in order, from the "coldest" to the "hottest." This takes a great deal of negotiation. Circulate, helping as needed. Students who have chosen the same word line up together.

   Note: In classes of more than fifteen students, several lines are formed.

6. Students call out their words. If necessary, they move to a different place in the line.

7. Each student makes up a sentence with the word and says the sentence aloud for everyone to hear. This is a chance for them to get feedback and correct their sentences.

Extension:

1. In small groups, students create a story using as many of the words as possible. Circulate to offer help on the target words only.

2. A secretary in each group writes the story.

3. In plenary, a student from each group reads the stories aloud.

Variation: The stories are posted on the walls around the room and students walk about reading the stories and commenting on them.

Note: Other domains that lend themselves well to this activity are: slow—fast, happy—sad, dirty—clean.

6.2   ACT IT OUT

James Asher's Total Physical Response (TPR) appeals to visual, aural, and kinesthetic learners, offers plenty of practice and immediate feedback about correctness, and is fun for students and teachers. It is an excellent way to introduce vocabulary and structures. It works well in large classes and is ideal for beginners. Who could ask for more?

This activity requires you to bring a list of actions to class. You may write this yourself or find excellent lists (as well as proven variations using TPR) in the resource books cited at the end of this activity.

LEVEL: Beginning—Intermediate

AIM: Vocabulary, structures, pronunciation

MATERIALS: A list of actions in a sequence

Procedure:

1.   Read aloud a sequence of actions, acting them out as you go. For example:

Climbing a Tree
>   Put on your old jeans.
>   Put on a good pair of shoes.
>   Find a good tree.
>   Climb up on the lowest branch.
>   Keep climbing up, higher and higher.
>   Don't look down!
>   Put your right foot on a thin branch.
>   Watch out! The branch is breaking!
>   You're falling!
>   Grab on with both hands.
>   Put your left foot on a thick branch.
>   Wait a minute.
>   Take a deep breath and calm down.
>   Climb up to the top of the tree.
>   Feel the gentle wind.
>   Smile.
>   Climb down carefully.

Note: With beginning students, use a short, simple sequence.

2. Read the sequence again, performing the actions. Students perform the actions along with you. This step may be repeated if necessary until most students are acting out your directions without looking at what their classmates are doing.

3. Read the sequence again, standing still this time. Students perform the actions as you read the sequence. Students who aren't sure what to do will look at classmates. This step, too, may be repeated.

4. Read the sequence again. Students repeat what you say chorally, again acting it out. Work on pronunciation and intonation as needed.

5. Give the words to students. Here are four ways to do this:
   a. Dictate the sequence. Encourage students to look at other papers as they write.
   b. Dictate to a student who writes at the board. The class calls out helpful suggestions and everyone copies the sequence as they go along.
   c. Send to the board as many pairs of students as you have sentences. Dictate one sentence to each pair, moving on quickly. (They will help each other remember the sentence.) In plenary, make corrections on the board before everyone copies the sequence into their notebooks.
   d. Write the sequence on the board yourself as students copy it down.

6. Pairs of students take turns reading and acting out the sequence.

Extension: Pairs come to the front to read and act out the sequence. They may even have it memorized by now.

References:

Seely et al., <u>TPR Is More Than Commands—At All Levels</u>. Berkeley, California, USA: Command Performance Language Institute, 1995.

G. Nelson and T. Winters, <u>Operations in English: 55 Natural Sequences for Language Acquisition</u>. Brattleboro, Vermont, USA: Pro Lingua Associates, 1993.

E. Romijn and C. Seely, <u>Live-Action English</u>. Hayward, California, USA: Alemany Press, a division of Janus Book Publishers, Inc., 1989.

6.3 MATCHING WORDS AND PICTURES

This activity allows students to choose words they want to learn. Pictures make the meanings clear and memorable.

LEVEL: Beginning—Intermediate

AIM: Learning new words

MATERIALS: A stack of old magazines, blank index cards

Procedure:

1. Hand out the magazines. Each student cuts out a picture of something he or she wants to learn the name of. (If you can't get magazines, students can draw a quick sketch instead.)

2. Collect these pictures and teach the names of the objects. (Students may help with this.) One way is to write the words on the board, showing the picture that corresponds to each word and leading the class in choral repetition of the words for pronunciation practice.

3. Set the pictures on the chalk shelf or tape them up where everyone can see them.

4. Hand out index cards and dictate one word to each student. They copy the word onto the blank card, checking the list of words on the board for correct spelling.

5. Students place these "word cards" next to the corresponding pictures.

6. Collect the cards and mix them up.

7. Students choose a new card and put it back with its picture, calling out the word as they do so.

8. Students make stories, using as many of the new words as possible.

9. They may:
   a. tell these to each other,
   b. write them and pass them around,
   c. post them on the walls and circulate, writing comments on others' papers.

Variations:

1. You can offer the mixed-up cards to students by tossing them onto your desk or by fanning them out like playing cards in your hands. Then have everyone come up, take one card, and put it back with its picture.

2. Alternatively, a volunteer can put all the cards back with their correct pictures. The rest of the students watch, offering help as needed.

3. If your class is large, choose fewer pictures to begin with. (Don't exceed ten to fifteen words.)

4. With large classes, students can work in groups. Each group cuts out a set of pictures. You circulate, helping with meaning and spelling. (Students will also be helping one another.)

Extension: Used regularly, this routine produces a growing collection of word cards. Collect sets of these in envelopes—e.g., foods, furniture, colors, places of business, etc. For literacy classes or pronunciation practice, use things that begin with *a*, *b*, *c*, etc. Mix all the sets; students re-sort them into their correct envelopes (with or without matching them with pictures).

6.4 WORDS ON A CHAIN

This is a good activity to use as a filler for the last ten minutes of class.

LEVEL: Intermediate—Advanced

AIM: Recycling vocabulary, spelling

Procedure:

1. The class stands in a circle.

2. Say any word—for example, "Bread."

3. The student next to you must produce a word that begins with the last letter of your word—for example, "Dance."

4. The procedure continues with the following student saying, for example, "End."

5. There is no waiting time. Students who don't immediately produce a word sit down.

6. The seated students catch as many words as they can while the game continues. They write as many sentences as they can while standing students continue the game.

7. When only one student is left standing, he or she is declared "Standing Winner."

8. Seated students read out their sentences.

9. The student with the most correct sentences is declared "Seated Winner."

Notes:

1. *In large classes, form standing rows instead of a circle and declare a row the winners when everyone in the other rows is seated.*

2. *For more challenge, limit the vocabulary to words in a certain domain—e.g., foods.*

6.5 GOING SHOPPING

This activity fosters concentration as it reinforces vocabulary.

LEVEL: Beginning—Intermediate

AIM: Recycling vocabulary, practicing the future with *going to*, practicing the verb *bought*.

Procedure:

1. Students sit in a circle of no more than fifteen. In large classes several circles are made.

2. Begin the chain by saying, "Today we are going to shop in a grocery store. I am going to buy apples."

3. The student on your right says, "The teacher (or your name) is going to buy apples. I am going to buy bread."

4. The next student says, "The teacher is going to buy apples. Iacovos is going to buy bread, and I am going to buy candy."

5. Continue around the circle. Each student adds a grocery item that begins with the next letter of the alphabet, and each student repeats all previous items. (You can skip the letters *q*, *x*, and *z*.)

6. When the circle has been completed, ask: "Who remembers what anyone bought?"

7. Volunteers speak. For example, "I remember that Alex bought sugar." "I remember that Francesca bought toilet paper."

Variation: You can, of course, also add furniture, clothes, or tools to your shopping list.

Extension: For more advanced students, have them write a short composition on "Why I Enjoy (Do Not Like) Shopping."

6.6 POINTING-OUT FUN

There is much laughter in the class while this activity proceeds.

LEVEL: Beginning—Low-Intermediate

AIM: Vocabulary review, practicing simple affirmative and negative sentences

Procedure:

1. Review all the objects in the room, including students' clothing and parts of the body.

2. Students stand and mingle. They approach another student. Standing close to an object, they point to it, saying, "This is a(n) . . ." and naming the object. Example: "This is a window."

   The student who has been approached responds, saying,

   "Yes, this is a window."

3. They stand near another object and reverse roles. The second student makes a statement, such as, "This is a nose," and is acknowledged by the first student, who says, "Yes, this is a nose."

4. Students move on to new partners and repeat the procedure. Allow them to continue in this way for about ten minutes.

5. Students continue as before, but this time they point to something and say that it is something else. For example, a student might point to another student's nose and say, "This is a foot." The partner's job is to say: "No, this is not a foot. This is a nose."

6. Continue this for about fifteen minutes. Students have great fun as they begin spontaneously tossing in other words they know, pointing to a desk, for example, and saying, "This is an elephant!"

Acknowledgment: We learned this from Tessa Woodward, at the Pilgrims' Language School in Canterbury, England.

6.7 I AM THE CURTAINS

This activity sparks imagination, generates vocabulary, and can give students a new way of seeing one another.

LEVEL: Intermediate—Advanced

AIM: Vocabulary, creativity

Procedure:

1. Ask students to look around the room and notice everything they see, from large features such as the ceiling to small things like a piece of chalk or the dust on a chair. (This can become a great opportunity for students to learn some new words from you and from classmates.)

2. Students tell you some of the things they have noticed. Note these on the board.

3. Ask students to relax and choose one thing that they feel some connection with.

   Write on the board:

   "I am the_____.
   I am . . . (adjective)
   I am . . . (another adjective)
   I have . . .
   I want . . .
   I never . . .
   I always . . .
   I like . . .
   I hate . . .
   I love . . .
   People _____ me . . .
   Nobody . . .
   I wish . . .
   Someday, . . ."

4. Demonstrate with any object in the room, calling on various students to offer statements using some of the prompts on the board.

   Example:

   "I am the curtains.
   I am dusty.
   I am old.

I let the light and heat inside every morning.
I keep the room cool in the afternoon.
I am very important.
People open me, close me, open me, close me every day.
But nobody notices me.
Nobody notices that I am dirty.
Nobody asks me what I want.
Someday I will refuse to slide.
Until they say, 'Thank you'."

5. Invite students to imagine that they are the object they chose. Ask them to mutter or whisper a long list of statements using the prompts on the board. (They may skip some prompts, use others more than once, or invent new ones.)

6. When they are ready, students write what they have created on paper.

7. Volunteers may read their sentences to the class.

Note: Don't tell the students in advance, but these are often revealing, personal poems. Students tend to project their own feelings onto the chosen object. For this reason it's important to let each student choose whether to read aloud.

6.8 FASHION SHOW

This activity appeals to students who like to perform.

LEVEL: Intermediate

AIM: Practicing the present continuous and the simple present, recycling vocabulary

Procedure:

1. Review clothing vocabulary by discussing what you and your students are wearing.

2. Review and write on the board vocabulary that describes clothing. For example:

"What can we say about a dress? That it is elegant, long, short, what color it is, how it is made, what kind of sleeves it has, whether or not it is comfortable, what kind of collar it has, what kind of buttons it has, what kind of neckline it has."

Do this with several items of clothing.

3. Choose a student as model and demonstrate the role of the announcer. Say, "Here comes Kumiko. She is wearing a pair of comfortable, stylish jeans and the latest model Arizona T-shirt. Notice the modern design of her T-shirt and nice fit of her jeans. The casual sneakers complete the ideal classroom outfit."

4. In pairs, students decide which will be the model and collaborate to write what the announcer will say.

5. They practice until the announcer feels comfortable in the role.

6. Pairs perform in front of the whole group. Students may set their papers aside and do this from memory if they wish.

6.9 POEMS FOR STUDENTS BY STUDENTS

This activity works well on a special day, such as Valentine's Day, the last day of class, or a student's birthday.

LEVEL: Intermediate—Advanced

AIM: Vocabulary expansion, writing, using parallel structures

Procedure:

Demonstration Phase

1. You and your students choose a famous person from current events or history. Example: John Fitzgerald Kennedy.

2. Write "John Fitzgerald" on the board. This becomes the first line of the poem your class will write.

3. Elicit adjectives that describe this person and with your class choose the three most appropriate adjectives to place under the name. Write these as the second line of your poem. Examples: "energetic, charismatic, handsome."

4. Elicit *ing* verb phrases from the class and together choose three that best suit the subject. Write these as the third line of your poem. Examples: "working with people, seeking advice, making decisions."

5. Elicit short sentences that describe the subject and with your class choose the most appropriate sentence to form the fourth line of the poem. Example: "He was our dream prince."

6. Add the last name, in this case "Kennedy," as the final line of the poem.

7. The poem on the board now reads:
    "John Fitzgerald
    Energetic, charismatic, handsome.
    Working with people, seeking advice, making decisions.
    He was our dream prince.
    Kennedy."

8. Several students read the poem aloud.

Production Phase

9. Students write their names on slips of paper.

10. Collect the slips and mix them.

11. Students choose one slip each.

12. In small groups, students help each other write poems about the students whose names they have chosen.

13. All poems are read aloud.

Caveat: Students should be told that their poems must reflect only positive qualities of their subjects.

Variations:

1. On the birthday of one student, the whole class can write poems to and about the person who is celebrating, while that student is assigned a composition on "The Ideal Birthday Celebration." At the conclusion of the lesson, all the poems as well as the composition are read aloud.

2. On Valentine's Day the final poems can be written up on hearts and given to each student as the class ends.

6.10 TWO-IN-ONE VOCABULARY REVIEW

In this word association game, the challenge of creating meaningful contexts for seemingly unrelated words activates students' imaginations. The new associations they create will help them remember vocabulary items.

LEVEL: Intermediate—Advanced

AIM: Vocabulary review, fluency

Procedure:

1. With your students, construct on the board a list of words to be reviewed.
2. Students form pairs.
3. Circle two unrelated words on the board.
4. Pairs quickly form a sentence using both words. When both partners of a pair agree on a sentence, they raise their hands together.
5. Call on either student from this first pair to say their sentence to the whole class.
6. Other pairs listen carefully and decide whether they have used the two words correctly.
7. If the sentence is incorrect, another pair may try.
8. Give a point to the first pair with a correct sentence.
9. Mark two more words and repeat the contest until all words have been used.

Note: Because students don't know which partner the teacher will call on, both partners in the pair must be ready to answer. You can encourage pairs to collaborate by subtracting a point when the partner you call on is unable to produce a sentence. Partners quickly learn to talk and listen fast to get each other ready.

Variations:

1. Have students do this alone, then compare their sentences with others in a noncompetitive lesson.
2. Put students in groups of three or more.

3. Increase the challenge level by circling three words instead of two. Students must use all three in a single sentence.

4. In large classes, divide the class into two teams. Successful sentences from pairs will score a point for their team.

6.11   TWO UNRELATED PICTURES

This activity makes a fine Friday reward activity when students have worked hard all week. They enjoy their classmates' creativity and surprise themselves with the novel associations they make as they discover what two unrelated pictures have in common.

LEVEL: Intermediate—Advanced

AIM: Generating new vocabulary, speaking

MATERIALS: A stack of magazines, some scissors (if available)

Procedure:

1. Students take magazines and cut out (or tear out) pictures that interest them. The number is not important; each student chooses one to four pictures.

2. Collect these and spread them all out on a desk or table or on the floor.

3. To demonstrate the activity, choose two large pictures that seem completely unrelated to each other. Hold these up and ask the class, "How are these pictures related? What is similar between them?" Be patient. If necessary, start by saying, "Well, they're both printed on paper!" to reassure students that you're not looking for a particular "right" answer. Students will soon offer their own ideas.

4. Divide students into groups of three: group A, group B, and group C.

5. A's come up and quickly choose two unrelated pictures.

6. A's return to their group and show B and C the pictures, asking, "How are these two pictures related?"

7. B and C come up with as many ideas as they can while A writes down a list of key words and phrases.

8. When they run out of ideas, B returns the pictures and chooses two new ones, repeating the game. (This time B writes the list.)

9. Finally, C gets a turn.

10. In plenary, each group gets up and shows their most interesting pair of pictures. They tell how these very different pictures are related. If time allows, students in the audience may offer more ideas about these two pictures.

11. As each group presents, write on the board useful words and phrases that come up. As you go along, ask whether these are new words for some students.

12. After each group presents, lead a round of applause for their creativity!

13. After all groups have presented, students practice the new words on the board.

Variation: If, over time, your picture collection grows to include some similar pictures, students can play "How Are These Different?"

Chapter Seven
Structure

Grammar is the glue that holds language together. A need for regularized patterning is a requirement for all human communication. It is grammar that helps us to decide who bit whom in the sentence, "Dog bit man." And it is grammar that tells us who is to treat whom and how in the sentence, "Be good to yourself."

Meanings, words, and social contexts all become clarified through appropriate structure. This is why we must not, in our quest for free and fluent communication, neglect the need for accurate structure. The activities in this chapter will help to introduce, practice, and reinforce grammatical patterns for our students.

7.1   RAINBOW TEAMS

This activity allows students to work at their own challenge level. In different lessons you can use this activity to review many different structures. It also provides plenty of feedback about correctness. The colored pens instantly let the teacher know who needs help and who can give help to others.

LEVEL: Beginning—Advanced

AIM: Grammar practice or comprehension check

Procedure:

1. Post large blank papers around the room.

2. Divide students into teams. (Pairs work well.)

3. Give each team a different-colored felt marker.

4. Dictate prompts. (See the examples that follow.) Students write one prompt at the top of each paper to get things started.

5. Teams circulate, visiting each paper and writing a response to each prompt.

6. When a significant error occurs, either help that team yourself or send someone from a team that is doing it correctly to help. (You will know, from the colors, who is doing it correctly.)

Note: Example prompts:

1. For a text students have read

a. Open-ended questions such as:
What did you like about this reading?
Not like?
Not understand?
Disagree with?
Agree with?
What else would you like to learn about this subject?

b. Sentence completions. (Dictate the beginnings of several sentences from the text, one for each paper.)

2. For grammar practice
Simple past (beginning level):

When I was a child . . .
Before I came to school here . . .
Last week . . .

Yesterday . . .
This morning . . .

Conditionals (intermediate level):

If I were rich . . .
If I were the teacher of this class . . .
If I had a motorcycle . . .
If I knew this new language perfectly . . .

Modals (advanced level): Ask students to create sentences using modals for a set of situations (one on each paper):

Your friend was in a car accident yesterday and has been having headaches since then.
Jun doesn't have a girlfriend.
Maria wants to pass the TOEFL. (or any major exam)
Masha needs a driver's license.
Wei Chen wants to give a dinner party.

7.2 GREAT ACCOMPLISHMENTS LINE-UP

This activity promotes lively discussion while students practice the present perfect tense.

LEVEL: Intermediate—Advanced

AIM: Practicing the present perfect tense, speaking

Procedure:

1. Together with students, make a list of inventions and/or accomplishments that have made our lives today easier. These can be personal, social, or historical accomplishments. Write these on the board using the present perfect tense—either in the active or the passive voice. For example:

   The telephone has been invented.
   The washing machine has been invented.
   The computer has been invented.
   I have learned to read.
   Yacovus has learned sixty new words.
   Ahmed has learned how to swim underwater with his eyes open.
   Theresa has learned how to bake a chocolate cake.
   The airplane has been invented.

2. Students choose one of these accomplishments. They may use an accomplishment not listed, but they must phrase it in the present-perfect tense.

3. Students stand and line up according to most important to least important accomplishments. Say, "The most important accomplishment is on the right; the least important is at the far end of the line, here on the left." Students will try to persuade one another as they line up. This is an exercise in compromise and requires a great deal of negotiation.

4. When the line-up is formed, students call out their "accomplishments" and explain how and why these accomplishments are important in their lives. For example: "The airplane has been invented. This is a great accomplishment for me because without the airplane I wouldn't be able to go home to my family for the holidays."

Variation: In classes larger than fifteen, students form several lines.

7.3 ALL IN A DAY'S WORK LINE-UP

This activity gives students a chance to think about how they organize their own time, while they review verb tenses. The story used in this example is for advanced students. You will, of course, adjust the number of verb tenses to the level of your class.

LEVEL: Intermediate—Advanced

AIM: Practicing tenses, speaking, writing

Procedure:

1. Before class starts, ask a student to copy the following chart on the board. Or create a similar chart with your students at the beginning of this activity. Or just photocopy it.

simple present	I dance.
present progressive	I am dancing.
simple past	I danced.
past progressive	I was dancing.
simple future	I will dance.
future progressive	I will be dancing.
present perfect	I have danced.
present perfect progressive	I have been dancing.
past perfect	I had danced.
past perfect progressive	I had been dancing.
future perfect	I will have danced.
future perfect progressive	I will have been dancing.

2. With your class, create a story about your friend Ellen. As you tell the story, write on the board all the verbs. Include with each verb a few words that come before or after the verb to give your students more memory cues. Be sure to write the verb in exactly the tenses you used as you told the story. Try to include as many tenses as possible in your story.

Example story:

(The underlined words are the ones you will write on the board.)

My friend Ellen got up at 5:00 o'clock this morning. She always gets up at 5:00 o'clock because she likes to take a long walk before breakfast. At 6:30, Ellen was already home. While Ellen was showering, the telephone rang. It was Ellen's mother, who had recently returned from a lovely vacation in the Bahamas, and she wanted to tell Ellen all about it. Ellen had never been to the Bahamas and she really wanted to hear all about it, but unfortunately she just didn't have time. She had to hurry to get to school. Ellen grabbed a quick breakfast and soon she was driving to school.

In class, Ellen worked hard: she explained, she wrote on the board, she listened and helped, she asked and answered questions, and she assigned work. When school was over, Ellen was looking forward to the rest of the day. She had planned to go to the theater with a good friend. "I have really done a lot today!" Ellen thought. "I deserve some fun!"

Ellen and her friend had dinner at their favorite restaurant. The two friends had known each other since they were in high school. They hadn't seen each other for some time, so they talked, and talked, and talked. "You know, we have been sitting here and talking for over two hours! I am really enjoying myself!" Ellen's friend said. "There is almost no sense in going to the theater. By the time we get there, they will have closed the doors," said Ellen. However, the friends hurried and they were lucky. When they got to the theater, the doors had not yet been closed.

3. Students choose any verb from the board.
4. Students line up according to the time order of Ellen's day. (This requires quite a bit of negotiation, as the past perfect actions happen before Ellen's day actually begins.)

Note: In classes of more than fifteen students, form several lines.

5. Students call out their verbs and explain which tense their verb is in and why that particular tense was used.

6. Students who are not in the right spot move to newly assigned spaces.

7. Students call out their verbs again.

8. Still in the line, students reconstruct the whole story.

Extension:

1. Sitting in small groups, students create their own stories, including as many tenses as possible. A secretary in each group writes the story.

2. A spokesperson from each group reads out the new story, and the class notes the tenses used. For example:

   Reader: "I have never eaten anything as delicious as fried octopus."

   Volunteer from class: "Have never eaten is the present perfect tense."

7.4 ON A SPECIAL DAY

This activity helps students to practice the problematic form of *on* + a day (*on my birthday*, etc.). Even very advanced students need to practice this bothersome point.

In multicultural classes, this activity also leads to interesting conversations about culture. Students don't notice the amount of practice they are getting, but it has its effect!

LEVEL: Intermediate—Advanced

AIM: Practicing the structure *on* a day as in *on Monday, on my birthday,* or *on the 6th of June*;" speaking

MATERIALS: A calendar that lists holidays

Procedure:

1. With the help of students, create a list on the board of special days in the country where you teach. In multicultural classes, get contributions from all the cultures represented. In the United States you might get: Christmas, Thanksgiving, Veterans' Day, Presidents' Day, Labor Day, Independence Day, Columbus Day, Easter, and Halloween. If many cultures are represented, you might also get Ramadan, Hanukkah, Rosh Hashana, Yom Kippur, Id al-fitr, Passover, Midsummer Day, Advent, the Day of the Dead, and Cinco de Mayo.

2. Together with your class, decide on which dates these days are celebrated. A volunteer student checks the calendar. (Certain holidays that follow a lunar calendar will have only approximate dates.)

3. Students choose one special day from the list.

4. Everyone calls out his or her day. If there are duplicates—for example, if everyone has chosen Christmas—some students will have to change their choice. This is an exercise in compromise.

5. Erase the list from the board.

6. Students line up according to when in the calendar year their days fall. January events are at the start of the line; December events at the end.

7. Each student calls out the name of his or her day and the date on which it is celebrated. For example, a student might say: "Christmas is celebrated on the 24th of December."

   If they are in the wrong place, they move.

8. Students talk with the person on their left about how they celebrate a special day.

9. Students tell the person on their right what they have been told by their previous partner.

7.5   "THERE IS NOTHING TO FEAR BUT FEAR ITSELF"

This activity allows students to practice the problematic form *to be afraid of.* The personal nature of this activity brings out some interesting talk and a lot of laughter. Students hardly notice how many times they are repeating the target structure.

The quotation of the title refers to President Franklin Delano Roosevelt's famous admonition to the American nation.

LEVEL: Intermediate—Advanced

AIM: Practicing *afraid of,* speaking, writing

Procedure:

1. Tell your class one of your own fears. Example, "I am afraid of mice."

2. Turn to a student and ask, "What are you afraid of, Mario?" and allow time for a response.

3. Motion to the student you have asked to ask another student.

4. Continue the procedure until all the students have spoken. As students speak, write the fears on the board.

5. Ask, "Who remembers the fear of someone else in the class?"

6. In plenary, listen to all responses. For example:

    "I remember that Kumiko is afraid of spiders." "I remember that Eva is afraid of illness."

7. Students choose one of the fears listed on the board. It should not be their own, and they should know whose it was.

8. Students call out the fear they have chosen together with the name of the student who mentioned it. For example, "Darkness: Reiko is afraid of darkness."

9. If several students have chosen the same fear, ask some to choose a different fear. This is an exercise in compromise.

10. If any student cannot remember who mentioned a particular fear, the class helps.

11. Students line up according to "size" or magnitude of the thing they are afraid of. This requires a great deal of negotiation and imagination as students decide the relative importance of "the dentist" or "darkness."

    Note: There will also always be students who are "afraid of nothing." The students must decide exactly where in the line this "nothing" fits best.

12. While standing in line, students call out who is afraid of what. Students at the beginning of the line name the "little" things, and this step proceeds to the "big" things at the other end of the line.

    Note: Students who feel that they are in the wrong place move. Students who are told by others that they are in the wrong place can either move or defend their place.

13. In plenary the class talks about the nature of fear and of phobias.

Extension: The class may write or talk about moments in history when fear or lack of fear influenced historical events.

7.6   VERBS ON A CHAIN

This activity encourages quick responses and helps to build automaticity in verb conjugations.

LEVEL: Intermediate—Advanced

AIM: Practicing both regular and irregular verbs

Procedure:

1. The class sits in a circle.
2. Appoint a scorekeeper.
3. All students write their first names on the board.
4. Say the infinitive form of an irregular verb. Example: "Eat."
5. The student next to you gives the past tense, "Ate."
6. The next student gives the past participle, "Eaten."
7. The following student produces a verb that begins with the last letter of the previous verb given. Example: "Need."
8. The chain continues. There is no waiting time—if the next response is not immediate, skip that student.
9. Everyone who produces a correct response gets a point. Irregular verbs get two points. Mistakes or hesitations earn a minus point. The scorekeeper writes the scores on the board.
10. Continue as long as the activity is moving briskly. Add up points and declare a winner.

Note: For large classes, do an initial demonstration circle and then set up several circles.

7.7   IF I MAKE A MILLION DOLLARS

This is a briskly paced activity that livens up a class while students practice a grammar point. It forces students to concentrate on content, vocabulary, and structure.

LEVEL: Intermediate—Advanced

AIM: Practicing *if*-clauses

Procedure:

1. Write on the board a sentence frame using *if* + the present tense—e.g., "If I _____, I will _____."

2. You and your students sit in a circle.

3. Say a hypothetical sentence like, "If I make a million dollars, I will travel around the world."

4. The first student to your right makes a sentence that uses your result clause as his or her *if*-clause—e.g., "If I travel around the world, I will stop in Rome."

5. The next student continues—e.g., "If I stop in Rome, I will go to the Vatican."

6. The chain might go around the circle one or more times, as long as student interest is high.

Notes:

1. *The final sentences are usually quite amusing and have nothing to do with the way the chain started.*

2. *This chain can of course be used with any if-clauses.*

3. *When the chain is finished, you can review the rules of if-clauses.*

7.8 TELL IT LIKE IT ISN'T

This activity produces a lot of laughter while students practice the present continuous.

LEVEL: Beginning—Low-Intermediate

AIM: Practicing the present continuous

Procedure:

1. Ask a student to come to the front of the class. Whisper to him or her to mime an action—for example, combing his or her hair.

2. As the student mimes, say, "I believe that Joanna is driving a car. Do you agree?"

3. Elicit from students, "No, she is not driving a car. She is combing her hair."

4. Ask another student to come to the front. Again, whisper a suggested action. (Possibilities: eating, drinking, brushing teeth, cooking, driving a car, knitting, sleeping, polishing nails, reading, writing a letter, turning on a faucet, washing dishes, taking a shower.)

Note: With beginners, list these verbs on the board.

5. As the student mimes, again suggest the wrong action and have the class correct you.

6. When the miming is done by a third student, elicit wrong information from a student and ask the class to correct it. For example, Jaime says, "I believe Maria is washing her hands." The class (watching Maria) objects: "No! She is combing her hair!"

7. Encourage students to use new verbs and continue the procedure as long as no one is bored.

7.9 BINGO

Bingo offers a game-like format to liven up repeated practice of structures and vocabulary recycling. Students discover that they must listen carefully in order to win.

LEVEL: Beginning—Advanced

AIM: Structure review, vocabulary review, listening

Procedure:

1. Draw a 9- or 16-square grid on the board.

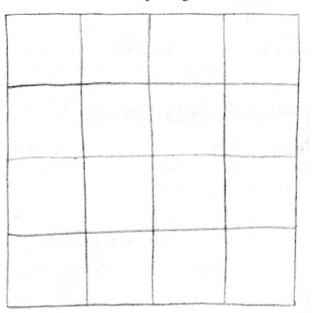

2. Students copy this onto papers.

3. Say to your students, "What are some words we want to review?" With your students, create a list of words on the board. (Do not write them in the grid you have made.)

4. Students write these in their grids in random order. (Every grid will have these words in a different arrangement.)

5. Call out the words one at a time. As students find a word in their grids, they cross it off. Call on volunteers to perform a task. Choose one task for your lesson. Possible tasks:

   For vocabulary review:

   a. Make sentences using the word correctly.

   For structure practice:

   b. Make questions using the word.
   c. Make negative sentences using the word.
   d. Make sentences using the word and also using a conjunction or a preposition you have written on the board.
   e. If all the words are verbs, make sentences using a particular tense.

6. As soon as any student has a vertical, horizontal, or diagonal straight line of crossed-out words, the student calls out, "Bingo!" If this lucky student can perform the assigned task correctly for all the words in his or her "Bingo" row, he or she is declared the winner. If not, the game continues until another student calls "Bingo!"

Note: To liven up a quiz, play Bingo and ask students to write their sentences instead of speaking them. Then collect the papers.

7.10 PERSONAL QUESTIONS

In this activity, students generate questions, then use them to get acquainted. It's fun because students get to decide which classmates they most want to interview.

LEVEL: Intermediate—Advanced

AIM: Question formation, getting acquainted, conversation

MATERIALS: A small box (approximately shoe-box size)

Procedure:

1. Say, "We're going to make up interesting questions to ask each other." For example:

   Who is your best friend? Tell me about him/her.
   Did you ever lose anything important? What happened?
   What is something good that happened to you recently?
   What would you like to be doing five years from now?

2. Students write more such questions. They bring their questions to you before putting them into the box. You may:

   point out errors and ask the writer to correct them,
   direct the writer to a classmate for help,
   correct errors yourself.

   Students who finish early write an extra question.

3. Once you have a few more questions in the box than there are students, the activity begins. Each student picks a question slip from the box. Everyone circulates with these questions, asking one classmate the question and having a short conversation.

   Note: Teach students the phrase "I'd rather not say" for questions they don't want to answer.

4. After students use their question one time, they come back to the box, redeposit that question, take a different question slip, and find a different partner to talk with.

5. Let the game continue for about twenty minutes.

6. In plenary, volunteers tell something interesting they learned about a classmate.

Variation: You may dictate (or develop with your class) a set of questions that require the use of a verb tense you have studied. Encourage students to help each other during the mingling phase by telling their partners, "Try again!" when errors are made.

7.11   CONJUNCTION CARDS

This activity is useful for introducing conjunctions and negative forms. The same activity can be used later as a review.

LEVEL: Intermediate—Advanced
AIM: Using conjunctions and negative forms
MATERIALS: Blank index cards

Procedure:

1. Choose a conjunction. Possible conjunctions include:
   and, but, or, nor, yet, so, because, although, however.

2. Give a few examples on the board of one conjunction joining parts of sentences. For example, if you have chosen *but*, write:

I like coffee
Toshi has a motorcycle } but { I don't like tea.
London is foggy

I like coffee · I don't like tea.
Toshi has a motorcycle · he doesn't have a car.
London is foggy · it isn't a bad place to live.

3. In plenary, invite volunteers to contribute a few more examples for the conjunction you have chosen.

4. Pairs of students create three sentences joined by the conjunction. For example, to practice *but*, students would make six cards that might look like this:

5. Circulate, checking these.

6. Students mix these up and give them to another pair.

7. Students re-match the mixed-up cards they have received, show these to the originating pair to confirm they have matched them correctly, write in the conjunction, and tape the sentences up around the room.

8. Everyone walks around, reading these aloud.

Variation: With more-advanced classes, add challenge by using not one, but two or three conjunctions at a time. If you write on the board, for example, *however, so, because*, student pairs might produce these six cards:

Reina works hard.

She never finishes her work.

I can't find my keys.

I can't drive my car.

I hate coffee.

It keeps me awake at night.

Note: The third example could use because or however, depending on one's attitude about being awake at night! If students have different opinions about how to re-match the sentences and which conjunctions to use, you have created a genuine speaking opportunity.

7.12 TRUTH, TRUTH, LIE

This activity stimulates imagination, encourages careful listening, and elicits genuine questions.

LEVEL: Intermediate—Advanced

AIM: Correct formation of questions

Procedure:

1. Write on the board three statements about yourself. Tell students that two statements are true and one is a lie. For example:

    "I once saw a bombing raid on Cairo, Egypt."
    "I know how to fly an airplane."
    "I have six brothers and sisters."

2. Every student writes three questions designed to find out more about your statements. For example:

    "When did you see the raid?"
    "What is an aileron?"
    "How old are all of your brothers and sisters?"

3. Classmates check to see that the questions are grammatically correct. Circulate, putting a checkmark by every correctly formed question.

4. Call on students quickly to ask you their questions. Smile but decline to answer incorrectly formed questions. Students take notes about your answers, calling for repetition if they don't hear or understand a question.

5. Any student who catches you in a contradiction or suspicious answer may challenge you. (Teach the phrase "I know what the lie is!" and write this on the board for use in the next round.)

6. If the student has discovered your lie and can explain why, confess and declare him or her the winner.

Extension: All students write three statements about themselves. Use these as the basis for further rounds of the game the same day or on succeeding days—in plenary or in pairs or groups.

7.13 NUMBERS IN MY LIFE

Students enjoy the guessing-game aspect of this activity.

LEVEL: Intermediate—Advanced

AIM: Practicing questions

Procedure:

1. Write on the board five or six numbers that are relevant in your life—for example, your shoe size, your age, the month you were married, the number of children you have, your telephone number, and your social security or identity card number.

2. Students ask you questions, trying to elicit what the numbers refer to. For example, "How old are you?"

3. After students have guessed as many numbers as they can, teach the rest. This becomes an interesting lesson in vocabulary and culture, as students learn what a social security number is.

4. Once the students know what your numbers refer to, they form groups of three and write down three of their own "secret numbers." They ask questions to guess one another's numbers.

7.14 PREFERENCES

This is a fine get-acquainted activity, which provides structure practice as well.

LEVEL: Intermediate

AIM: Practicing comparative forms of adjectives, question formation, third-person singular verbs, present tense, recycling vocabulary

Procedure:

1. Across the top of a paper each student writes these pairs of column headings:

   Summer, Winter
   Sun, Rain
   Sunday, Monday
   Chocolate, Strawberries

2. If class is large, put students in groups of five or six.

3. Down the left side of the paper, each student makes a vertical list of the first names of all classmates. Students draw lines to form a grid.

	Summer	Winter	Sun	Rain	Sunday	Monday	Chocolate	Strawberries
Tomoko								
Elizabeth								
Jae-Lee								
Ahmed								
Marcella								
Mohammed								
Jose								
Jung-Hee								
Pierre								
Awa								
Hirohito								

4. Students mingle, asking each other questions—for example: "Do you prefer summer to winter? Why do you prefer winter?" They briefly note their classmates' answers in the proper space on their grid.

5. In plenary, students report their findings to the class. Example: "Danuta prefers strawberries to chocolate because strawberries taste better and they don't make her fat."

7.15   SENTENCE CONTRACTION

This exercise helps students figure out long, difficult sentences by finding the "skeleton" of a sentence.

LEVEL: Intermediate—Advanced

AIM: Understanding long sentences, practicing grammatical structures

Procedure:

1. Put a long sentence on the board, from your imagination or from your text. For example:

   "My grandmother, who lived in New York, smoked an expensive little cigar every afternoon of her life but, in spite of this dirty, dangerous habit, lived to be eighty-six years old."

2. Ask students, "What can we remove and still have a correct sentence?"

3. Each time a student calls out a suggestion, put parentheses around that word or phrase.

4. The class reads aloud what is left (omitting what is in parentheses) and decides whether this is still a grammatically possible sentence.

5. If the deletion works, erase it.

6. Continue the procedure, calling on students until the sentence is as sparse as it can be. Feel free to change words a bit to get down to the absolute "skeleton" of the sentence. For example, your class might end with, "My grandmother smoked cigars but lived to be old."

Note: There is usually more than one way to trim a sentence down to its basic elements. Exploring these can lead students to greater facility with the many ways to express ideas in their new language.

Variation:

1. When you are studying a particular grammatical structure, ask students to write on the board several sentences, all containing the same grammatical structure.

2. In plenary, make any necessary corrections.

3. Ask students to read out the sentences without and with the target structure. For example, in a lesson on adjective clauses, these two sentences might be on the board:

"Dini likes coffee that comes from Brazil."
"People who drive too fast have accidents."

Students will say,

"Dini likes coffee."
"People have accidents."
"People who drive too fast have accidents."

Try this with other clauses, with prepositional phrases, with adjectives and adverbs.

Doing this is an effective way to practice the target structure, and the drill remains interesting because the sentences come from the students themselves.

7.16 SENTENCE EXPANSION

This exercise helps students write more interesting sentences. It's also a very effective way to practice many grammatical structures.

LEVEL: Intermediate—Advanced

AIM: Adding "richness" to writing, practicing structures

Procedure:

1. Put a simple sentence on the board—for example, "Salem does homework." Leave plenty of space between the words.

2. Ask students what they can add to this sentence. You may accept all offerings, or you may ask for particular structures.

3. Students who want to add something say the whole sentence, including their addition.

4. Ask the class whether this addition is grammatically possible. If it is, write it in (or invite a student to do this). This step is the heart of the activity. Students explore what can and cannot be done with a sentence.

5. Continue the activity, accepting contributions until the sentence is stretched to ridiculous lengths. If students run out of ideas too soon, prompt them from this list: Where? When? Why? How? How many? How much? What kind of? How often? Who else? What else?

Variation: To target a particular structure:

1. Put several simple sentences on the board.

2. Students add the target structure to each sentence.

3. In plenary, make any necessary corrections.

4. Ask students to read the sentences without and with the target structure. For example, in a lesson on prepositional phrases, you might have these sentences on the board:

"Miki gave Matteo a pencil."
"A woman smiled at Chantal."
After adding prepositional phrases, students say:
"Miki gave Matteo a pencil. Miki gave Matteo a pencil <u>with no eraser</u>."
"A woman smiled at Chantal. A woman <u>in a red car</u> smiled at Chantal."

TO THE INDEXES . . .

INDEX OF ROUTINES

> Please see the section dealing with routines on page x in the Introduction. Briefly, a "routine," as we are using the term in this book, is an activity so effective that you use it again and again, varying the content and challenge level but keeping the same basic steps.
>
> Here are some of the routines we often use. Each has variations; you will doubtless think of other ones!

Routine 1: Brainstorm

Students generate ideas rapidly while a "secretary" records them. All ideas are accepted without discussion or judgment.

3.4   The World Out There 18
3.6   Building Up a Chain: Rules to Live By 22
4.2   What We Already Know 42
7.5   "There Is Nothing to Fear but Fear Itself" 105

Routine 2: Change the Format

Students change prose to a chart, narration to a time line, a paragraph to a poem, a picture to a paragraph, etc.

4.13   Change the Format 52

Routine 3: Chains

Students pass on information to other students. Sometimes they expand on the information, sometimes change it in some way, and sometimes collect other students' information as it flows along the "chain" of students.

1.1   Clearing the Decks 2
3.6   Building Up a Chain 22
3.10   This Makes Me Think of That..............................26
3.14   Gossip 29
5.12   Countries, States, and Cities 72
6.4   Words on a Chain 88
6.5   Going Shopping 89
7.4   On a Special Day..104
7.6   Verbs on a Chain 107
7.7   If I Make a Million Dollars 107

Routine 4: Concentric Circle Talk

Students form two concentric circles. Each student in the inner circle faces a partner in the outer circle. They tell (or sometimes exchange) information with partner after partner. The outer circle moves one place to the right after each turn.

3.12   Concentric Circle Talk...27

Routine 5: Cloze

Any reading passage with blanks in it is a cloze.

5.6   Missing Words Dictacomp 63
5.18   Cloze Dictation 79

Routine 6: Continuums

A range between two extremes along which students can take a stand is a continuum.

3.17   Continuums 32
6.1   From Cold to Hot...84

Routine 7: Dictacomp

This is a combination of dictation and composition in which students reconstruct or paraphrase a passage for which they have some key words.

2.1   Dictacomp for Listening 8
5.2   The Classic Dictacomp 59
5.3   Student-to-Student Dictacomp 60
5.4   Group-to-Group Dictacomp 61
5.5   Acting-Out Dictacomp 62
5.6   Missing Words Dictacomp 63

Routine 8: Interaction Lines

This routine allows students to familiarize themselves with the ideas in a piece of text and then to create and drill questions about these ideas.

3.16   Interaction Lines 31

Routine 9: Line-Ups

A negotiation activity in which students stand in line in a particular order, depending on time (sequence of events), intensity of feelings, or relative importance of ideas in the context of a lesson.

3.11   The Birthday Line...26
6.1   From Cold to Hot...84
7.2   Great Accomplishments Line-Up...101

7.3   All in a Day's Work Line-Up 102
7.4   On a Special Day...104
7.5   "There Is Nothing to Fear but Fear Itself" 105

Routine 10: Rainbow Teams

Students write responses with colored felt markers, getting instant feedback on their work from classmates and/or the teacher.

7.1   Rainbow Teams 100

GENERAL INDEX OF ACTIVITIES

Activities that Appeal to Varied Intelligences

These activities engage "intelligences" other than the strictly verbal, including artistic, musical, and kinesthetic intelligences.

2.4   Students in Charge of Listening 9
2.5   Picture Dictation 10
2.7   Singing Dictation 12
3.10   This Makes Me Think of That...26
3.18   Role-Plays 33
3.19   Categories 35
3.20   What Machine Am I? 36
3.22   Four Pictures Make a Story 38
5.1   Three Unrelated Things...58
5.5   Acting-Out Dictacomp 62
5.13   Remember the Picture 73
5.20   Faces 80
6.2   Act It Out 85
6.3   Matching Words and Pictures 87
6.7   I Am the Curtains 91
6.8   Fashion Show 92
6.9   Poems for Students by Students...93
6.11   Two Unrelated Pictures 96

Beginning-Level Activities

Most of the activities in this book are presented as suitable for Intermediate—Advanced. Many of these can easily be used at lower levels if the teacher controls content and vocabulary.

We have indexed here those activities that as described in the book are already suitable for beginning classes.

1.5   Paying Compliments 4

1.6   What I Like to Eat...5

2.1   Dictacomp for Listening 8

2.2   Reconstruct the Story 8

2.5   Picture Dictation 10

2.6   Story with Mistakes 11

2.7   Singing Dictation 12

3.7   Homework Review I: Seek and Find 23

3.8   Homework Review II: Homework Pairs 25

3.9   Homework Review III: Stand and Deliver 25

3.12   Concentric Circle Talk 27

3.14   Gossip 29

4.1   Predicting from the Title 42

4.2   What We Already Know 42

4.5   Classic Jigsaw..45

4.17   Quick-Skim 56

5.2   The Classic Dictacomp 59

5.3   Student-to-Student Dictacomp 60

5.5   Acting-Out Dictacomp 62

5.8   Revision: I Can Do It Myself...65

5.10   Peer Revision II: Editing Written Work in Pairs.......................68

5.15   Gift Exchange 75

5.18   Cloze Dictation 79

6.2   Act It Out 85

6.3   Matching Words and Pictures 87

6.5   Going Shopping 89

6.6   Pointing-Out Fun *(beginning only)*..90

7.1   Rainbow Teams 100

7.8   Tell It Like It Isn't 108

7.9   Bingo...109

Class Cohesion Activities

These activities help students to know classmates better.

1.1   Clearing the Decks 2

1.2   My Adjective 3

1.3   People We Admire 3

1.4   The First Time...4

1.5   Paying Compliments 4

1.6   What I Like to Eat...5

3.1   Find Someone Who 14

3.2   Candy Exchange 16

3.3   What I Need 16

3.5   I'm in Charge of My Own Learning 20

3.6   Building Up a Chain: Rules to Live By 22
3.7   Homework Review I: Seek and Find 23
3.8   Homework Review II: Homework Pairs 25
3.11   The Birthday Line 26
3.20   What Machine Am I? 36
5.9   Peer Revision I: What I Think You Said.............................69
5.15   Gift Exchange 75
5.16   Who Is This? 77
5.17   Buddy Journals 77
6.5   Going Shopping (good for remembering classmates' names) 89
6.7   I Am the Curtains 91
6.9   Poems for Students by Students.......................................93
7.5   "There Is Nothing to Fear but Fear Itself" 105
7.10   Personal Questions 110
7.12   Truth, Truth, Lie 113
7.13   Numbers in My Life 114
7.14   Preferences..115

Community

These activities use the community beyond the classroom.

3.3   What I Need 16
3.4   The World Out There 18
3.5   I'm in Charge of My Own Learning 20
3.18   Role-Plays 33
3.21   Real Language 37

Discussion Starters

These activities provide lively conversation.

1.2   My Adjective 3
1.3   People We Admire 3
1.4   The First Time...4
3.1   Find Someone Who 14
3.3   What I Need 16
3.11   The Birthday Line 26
3.17   Continuums 32
3.18   Role-Plays 33
3.21   Real Language 37
4.12   Find a Sentence 51
5.11   Quick-Write 70
5.14   Written Argument 74
5.20   Faces 80
7.2   Great Accomplishments Line-Up.......................................101

7.5   "There Is Nothing to Fear but Fear Itself" 105
7.12   Truth, Truth, Lie 113
7.13   Numbers in My Life 114

Energizers

These activities lift the energy level of a class.

2.7   Singing Dictation 12
3.1   Find Someone Who 14
3.3   What I Need 16
3.10   This Makes Me Think of That...................................26
3.11   The Birthday Line 26
3.12   Concentric Circle Talk...................................27
3.16   Interaction Lines 31
3.17   Continuums 32
3.19   Categories 35
5.5   Acting-Out Dictacomp 62
5.11   Quick-Write 70
5.15   Gift Exchange 75
6.2   Act It Out 85
6.4   Words on a Chain 88
6.5   Going Shopping 89
7.6   Verbs on a Chain 107
7.7   If I Make a Million Dollars 107
7.8   Tell It Like It Isn't 108
7.9   Bingo...................................109
7.10   Personal Questions 110
7.15   Sentence Contraction 116
7.16   Sentence Expansion...................................117

Preview Activities

Many of these activities work equally well for review and so are indexed under "review" as well.

2.1   Dictacomp for Listening 8
2.2   Reconstruct the Story 8
3.6   Building Up a Chain: Rules to Live By 22
3.12   Concentric Circle Talk...................................27
3.13   The Unfinished Story 28
3.15   Two-Minute Presentations 30
3.18   Role-Plays 33
4.1   Predicting from the Title 42
4.2   What We Already Know 42
4.3   Tell a Tale of Guesswork 43

4.4	Preteaching Vocabulary	44
4.5	Classic Jigsaw	45
4.6	Paragraph Jigsaw	46
4.8	Vocabulary Jigsaw	48
4.9	Predicting from Sentences	49
4.15	Reading with Half the Words	54
4.17	Quick-Skim	56
5.2	The Classic Dictacomp	59
5.3	Student-to-Student Dictacomp	60
5.4	Group-to-Group Dictacomp	61
5.5	Acting-Out Dictacomp	62
5.6	Missing Words Dictacomp	63
5.7	Sentence-by-Sentence Dictacomp	64
5.11	Quick-Write	70
5.14	Written Argument	74
5.18	Cloze Dictation	79
7.15	Sentence Contraction	116
7.16	Sentence Expansion	117

Pronunciation

Many of the activities in this book can be used to focus on pronunciation; the following have pronunciation as a primary focus.

2.7	Singing Dictation	12
3.14	Gossip	29
4.7	Question Jigsaw	47
4.14	Telling Back and Forth	53
5.4	Group-to-Group Dictacomp	61
5.9	Peer Revision I: What I Think You Said	67
5.16	Who Is This?	77
6.2	Act It Out	85
6.3	Matching Words and Pictures	87

Review Activities

Many of these are also suitable for preview.

2.1	Dictacomp for Listening	8
3.6	Building Up a Chain: Rules to Live By	22
3.7	Homework Review I: Seek and Find	23
3.8	Homework Review II: Homework Pairs	25
3.9	Homework Review III: Stand and Deliver	25
3.12	Concentric Circle Talk	27
3.15	Two-Minute Presentations	30
3.16	Interaction Lines	31

3.18   Role-Plays 33
4.5   Classic Jigsaw...45
4.11   Student-Made Tests 50
4.12   Find a Sentence 51
4.16   Overhead Summaries...55
5.2   The Classic Dictacomp 59
5.3   Student-to-Student Dictacomp 60
5.4   Group-to-Group Dictacomp 61
5.5   Acting-out Dictacomp...62
5.9   Peer Revision I: What I Think You Said................67
5.11   Quick-Write 70
5.14   Written Argument 74
5.19   One-Minute Feedback 79
6.10   Two-in-One Vocabulary Review 95
7.6   Verbs on a Chain 107
7.9   Bingo...109
7.11   Conjunction Cards 111

Settling-down Activities

After students have been up and involved, these two activities help them to quiet down.

2.5   Picture Dictation 10
3.15   Two-Minute Presentations.....................................30

Short Activities

These activities work well as lesson starters.

1.2   My Adjective 3
1.3   People We Admire 3
1.4   The First Time..4
1.5   Paying Compliments 4
1.6   What I Like to Eat..5
2.3   Announcements..9
4.1   Predicting from the Title 42
4.2   What We Already Know 42
4.17   Quick-Skim..56
5.11   Quick-Write 70
6.4   Words on a Chain 88

Quick Notes

Quick Notes

Quick Notes

Quick Notes

Quick Notes

Quick Notes

Quick Notes

Quick Notes

Quick Notes

Quick Notes

Quick Notes

Quick Notes

Quick Notes